ITALY BEFORE
THE ROMANS

MODEL OF A HOUSE FROM THE FORUM, ROME

ITALY BEFORE
THE ROMANS

By DAVID RANDALL-MacIVER

COOPER SQUARE PUBLISHERS, INC.
NEW YORK   1972

Originally Published 1928 by
Oxford University Press
Reprinted by Permission of Oxford University Press
Published 1972 by Cooper Square Publishers, Inc.
59 Fourth Avenue, New York, N. Y. 10003
International Standard Book No. 0-8154-0426-3
Library of Congress Catalog Card No. 76-145874

Printed in the United States of America

CONTENTS

LIST OF ILLUSTRATIONS

The frontispiece has been supplied by the Director of the Forum Excavations. The figures in Plates 1 and 2 are selected from Montelius, *La civilisation primitive en Italie.* The figures in plates 4, 5, 8 are selected from *Villanovans and Early Etruscans;* the remainder are from *The Iron Age in Italy.*

ITALY BEFORE
THE ROMANS

INTRODUCTION

Historians have deliberately kept silence as to all Italian peoples except the Roman. But it is obvious that the view which they give is incomplete. The Romans were not a highly civilized people in the early days of the Republic. Italy was completely civilized before its conquest by Rome. Archaeology can give a picture of the life of Italian peoples scarcely known to history.

THOSE who have studied Roman history in the pages of such a writer as Mommsen, or in the original annals of Livy and Polybius, must often have reflected that they have learned very little of any Italian people except the Romans. Etruscans, Samnites, Picenes, and scores of less familiar tribes appear sporadically in the record of wars and struggles, but they are empty names without form or content. It is natural enough, because these historians never set themselves any aim except that of describing the rise and development of a single great nation, which was of supreme importance in the evolution of the ancient and the modern world. Such intense absorption in a single theme produces its inevitable effect. The reader closes his Livy with precisely that impression which the great advocate and patriot undoubtedly meant to convey. For him the Romans were the chosen people, who in the teeth of unrighteous opposition forced the blessings of an incomparable civilization by dint of ceaseless effort upon a number of barbarous Gentiles, who happened to share the peninsula with them.

Yet an unbiassed student can easily realize that this conception must be very far from the truth. No doubt a Roman in the days of Augustus was, or could be, an exceedingly polished person. The wisdom of Greek poets and philosophers, the art of Oriental and Hellenic craftsmen, the science of Egypt and Syria, all the resources of the contemporary world were at his disposal if he cared to use them. True that he might not care; the perennial Philistine was always there, as he is in all countries, though his name has fortunately perished. But no one can question the general level of taste and cultivation in a public that could appreciate the poets of the Augustan era and the sculptures of the Ara Pacis.

Nevertheless, the Roman of three or four centuries earlier was a very different person. When Greece was still unknown and the treasures of Etruscan cities were unpillaged, when even Ennius had not begun to write and the native literature was unborn, no one could call the Roman civilized. In the fourth century or the fifth he was extremely backward compared with several other nations in Italy. The Senate that awed ᵗhe invading Gauls may have been a very reverend assembly, but it was composed of exceedingly rude fore-fathers of the hamlet. Incessantly occupied with the wars which were necessary to ensure their mere existence as a state, the Romans had had no time even if they possessed the inclination to culti-vate the arts and amenities of life. A Cato could recognize this and take pride in it; but his self-righteousness naturally forbade him to admit that the civilization of his enemies might be superior to his own. The loss of Cato's *Origines* matters very little to us.

No written documents in fact exist, or ever existed, from which we could learn the facts that archaeology clearly teaches. It is only as the result of exploration on the sites of forgotten cities and cemeteries that the splendid civilizations have been made known, which reached their zenith in all the provinces of Italy long before these came under Roman domination. Before they were compelled to submit to the organizing and levelling control of the central capital Etruria, Venetia, Lombardy, Picenum, and perhaps even Apulia, had each evolved its own independent and very valuable culture. And at the same time the whole of the south from Naples to Brindisi had been civilized by the spread of Corinthian and Ionic art.

Rome, when she conquered and annexed these territories, became heir to a fully developed estate.

Italy had been created, but it had been created by others; the task that fell to the Romans was much more suited to their peculiar abilities, they had to organize and administer the country. But it was a country fully reclaimed from the wild, inhabited not by barbarous aborigines but by a series of peoples most of whom were highly civilized and fully able to educate their political masters. Agriculture was practised on a large scale, wealthy and important cities had existed for centuries, an extensive foreign commerce had long been conducted both by land and sea, not only with the Mediterranean but with distant ports of Continental Europe. The houses of Etruscans and Venetians, Capuans and Cumaeans, were full of objects of art and luxury of which the very names were unknown to the Romans of the early republic.

Archaeology is powerless of course to recount the exploits of the heroes who 'lived before Agamemnon', but it can paint a picture of the scenes in which they lived and moved. It can give us some idea of the greatness of the men even though their individual names have perished. And if there are still scholars who protest that such things are not worth knowing, they can no longer have any excuse for asserting them to be unknowable.

It is from the results of the great mass of archaeological discoveries made in Italy during the last seventy years that I shall try to construct a char-

acterization of the chief peoples who may be styled
the Forerunners of the Romans.[1]

[1] In a small book intended for the general reader it has
seemed desirable to avoid all foot-notes and references.
The student who cares to examine and review for himself
the facts upon which I have built my inferences will find
them in the three following works, all published by the
Clarendon Press, Oxford:

The Stone and Bronze Ages in Italy, by T. E. Peet.
Villanovans and Early Etruscans, by D. Randall-MacIver.
The Iron Age in Italy, by D. Randall-MacIver.

CHAPTER 1

The Neolithic Age

Race-elements in south and east of Italy the same now as in the Neolithic Age. Effects of invasion in changing population of north and west. Geographic conditions in Neolithic times. Original settlement by the Mediterranean Race. Routes by which this race entered Italy. Permanence of the Mediterranean Race as an element. Contrast between eastern and western halves of the Mediterranean world about 2500 B.C. General picture of life in Italy at this date. Neolithic dwellings. Pottery making. Stone implements.

ITALY did not begin to enter into the full current of European life, and to share the activities and commerce of the awakening western world, until about 1600 B.C. This is the time when the Bronze Age is in full swing, and a general level of uniform culture has spread over all Europe, from the Danube to the Baltic and from Spain to the British Isles. From that date onwards the early history of Italy becomes a chapter in the general history of Europe. But we must go back fully a thousand years before this to study the original conditions which differentiated the Italians from their neighbours, and invested them with a special and peculiar individuality.

The main outlines in the distribution of the population were determined as early as the Neolithic Age, and over a great part of the country they have never been changed since that time. Essentially the same race inhabits the entire south and most of the east of Italy to-day which settled there several thousand years before Christ. But the north and west have been profoundly affected by a series of immigrations and invasions, which began with the very dawn of the Bronze Age. These invasions brought with them the seeds of new development, and were a principal factor in the evolution of the country. Nevertheless, it must not be supposed that they were indispensable for its progress ; the introduction of new races was rather a geographical incident than a biological necessity. The Mediterranean stock always possessed unlimited potentialities, and could perfectly have worked out its own salvation without calling in other peoples. The history of the Aegean affords ample proof of this.

In considering the earliest settlement of the peninsula we may leave out of account the hard-living hunters of the Old Stone Age, who picked up a precarious living in the immeasurably distant lifetime of the elephant and cave-bear. These formed only a very tiny proportion of the eventual population, and had almost no effect on its progress and development. In their day the continent of Europe was still attached to Africa; two great land-bridges united Spain with Morocco on the one side, and Tunis with Sicily and Calabria on the other. The Mediterranean was not a sea but only an inland lake. But all this had changed before Neolithic times; the land-masses and the seas had everywhere assumed the general contour which they show to-day; and the conditions of climate had settled down to very much the same that they are in our own time. It is possible to think of the Neolithic world in terms of modern thought, without exercising our retrospective fancy in the realm of palaeontology. Neolithic man, in whatever part of Europe he may be studied, had everywhere arrived at a stage of life which is perfectly intelligible to the modern mind. Already he lived in artificially constructed dwellings, grouped in communities which presuppose a high degree of social organization. Nomadism had been abandoned, the hunting-man of the older Stone Age had either vanished or been converted to new ways. Agriculture, the farming of stock, and the exercise of simple industries like pottery-making and weaving, produce the impression of an existence which may be called primitive but is by no means squalid. The general level is that of the happy savage, who has existed in unspoiled parts of the world like the Pacific down to the memory of many who are still living.

In Italy it is the Neolithic men who may be considered for all practical purposes as the aborigines. Their predecessors of Palaeolithic times doubtless left a certain number of descendants, whose survival can be traced here and there in the subsequent period. But these were comparatively few and unimportant. The first permanent and universal settlement of the peninsula was made some thousands of years before Christ, by a variety of that species which has been named the Mediterranean Race, because it is found distributed all round the borders of the Mediterranean from Spain to the Levant. It is a large species with many varieties, which had become differentiated, during the Quaternary period in some part of Africa north of the tropical belt. The need for expansion forced it outwards in all directions until it occupied all the shores of the Mediterranean on both sides, as well as the larger islands.

The immigration into Italy followed two distinct routes, corresponding to the old land-bridges, though these no longer existed. One large body, destined to form the aboriginal population of all North and Central Italy, crossed by the Straits of Gibraltar and passed up the east coast of Spain and along the Riviera. Their path can be traced by the products and remains of their graves and habitations, which are so precisely similar as to make it certain that they belong to a single movement. Archaeologists have agreed to call this people the Ibero-Ligurians, which is a very appropriate name as it recalls their ethnical origin and affinities. The second route was along the line of the old eastern land-bridge, at this time broken down into a chain of headlands and islands, leading by way of Sicily into the modern Calabria. Inasmuch as the Neolithic civilization of Southern Italy shows many minor points of difference from that of the north it has been generally agreed to give a separate name to its representatives, though it must not be supposed that they are anything but a sub-variety, differing very little in essential character from the Ibero-Ligurians. In view of their close connexion with Sicily we may term them Siculans.

The Neolithic race which entered the country from both ends at this remote period has remained undisturbed in many regions down to the present day, and has always constituted a numerical majority of the whole Italian people. It may be remarked in passing that it was one of the three elements which combined to form Rome itself, and was probably the most durable of the three. On the east of the Apennines the descendants of the Ibero-Ligurians successfully resisted all attempts at invasion during the Bronze and Early Iron Ages; and under the Roman domination continued in exclusive possession of half the Adriatic coast, as well as of a large part of the mountainous interior. Their most powerful and important representatives in later times are the Picenes and Samnites of the historians.

In North Italy and on the west of the Apennines the Neolithic race was subdued during the second millennium B.C. by invaders of wholly different origin, but though dominated and overshadowed it remained a by no means negligible element. South of Naples, on the other hand, the Mediterranean Race has always been not only the principal but the only factor in the population, except for such alien elements as may have come in with the Greek colonies. It was possibly reinforced from time to time by overflows from Sicily, but there is evidence to show that these must have ceased before 1000 B.C. Even before the Bronze Age Sicily and Italy had become two wholly distinct provinces, each deriving its inspiration from a perfectly different source.

We may now attempt to construct a general picture of Italian life as it appeared about 2500 B.C., when the settlement of the country had been completed, probably two or three thousand years after it had begun, though it is not possible to state this with accuracy.

The contrast between the eastern and western halves of the Mediterranean world at this date is very striking. Egypt, Mesopotamia, Crete, and Anatolia have reached almost the zenith of their civilization. In Egypt is the time of the Old Empire, with its magnificent buildings, unequalled sculpture, beautiful painting, and exquisite minor arts. In Crete the Early Minoan is entering on its third phase; the period of the great palaces has not quite begun, but the existence of well-planned cities and powerful navies shows a highly organized state with all the complexity and the implied refinement of a most sophisticated life. In comparison with these eastern countries Europe seems to be peopled by savages. Between an Egyptian noble and a tribal chief in France or Italy of this period there must have been as much difference as between Sir Walter Raleigh and an American Indian of the sixteenth century. Yet if we turn our eyes away from the dazzling picture of Oriental empires, and measure Neolithic Europe by less exacting standards, it will appear that the Europeans have really made immense advances and have placed their feet some way up on the ladder of progress. If the Europeans are fully a thousand years behind the natives of the Near East, this is not due to any inherent incapacity but only to geographical conditions, and the comparative isolation which these had entailed. Once communications are opened up the development will be rapid, and before the middle of the second millennium B.C. an era of remarkable progress will begin; this will be the theme of my second chapter.

About 2500 B.C., then, we find that Italy is sufficiently, though not densely, populated from

end to end with a people of Eur-African origin
belonging to the Mediterranean Race. Though
distantly related to such remarkable stocks as the
Cretan and the Minoan Greeks, the Italians are
very imperfectly developed in regard to material
culture. They have been settled for many centuries in the peninsula, but still retain many
characteristics which recall their origin and their
wanderings from Africa through Spain and Sicily.
Their habits of life at this time were principally
pastoral. Hunting, however, was not neglected,
and was the more necessary because agriculture
was only in its infancy, even if it had begun at all,
which is doubtful. Bones of wild animals found
in their dwellings show that this people hunted
the stag, bear, fox, wolf, wild-boar, and hare.
This is a list which may give some idea of the
character of the country-side, evidently densely
forested, probably in the main with oak and chest-
nut.

In this virgin forest the aborigines were making
clearings, in which they built wattle huts and reared
their domestic animals. For already the sheep,
the goat, the horse, the ox, ass, and pig had been
domesticated. The dog does not seem to have
been tamed as yet, and it is only some centuries
later that he becomes a partner in the daily life.
Grinding-stones have been found, but it must not
be assumed that they were used for any kind of

cultivated grain. Neolithic man in Italy had probably to be content with flour made from acorns
and chestnuts, and with the pounded seeds of wild
plants.

His dwellings were very primitive. In some parts
of the country caves were the principal if not the
only habitations, but in others have been found
the remains of wattle-and-daub huts, which may
be considered as more genuinely characteristic of
the period. The general form of these huts may
be inferred from pottery models—actually 1,500
years later—found in the Alban hills, in the
Forum at Rome, and on many Tuscan sites (see
Frontispiece). If slightly improved they preserve
the old style and tradition, being round or elliptical in shape, constructed of clay-daubed wattle
and posts and roofed with rough-hewn beams.
They were generally grouped into hamlets or
small villages, large enough to contain several
families but hardly more.

Dwellings of this kind can be remarkably com-
fortable if they are well kept. I have seldom been
better housed on any exploring expedition than
in a series of wattle huts set up to form a country
hotel in a newly settled part of South Africa. But,
of course, the huts of these primitive aborigines
were not well kept. Neolithic man was very
untidy in his habits, and his wife had scarcely
learned the modern technique of housekeeping.

This is fortunate for the student, as otherwise we should have known very little of the life of the time. For almost all our information is actually derived from the rubbish, and the more or less accidental deposits of weapons and implements, which were buried or lost in the refuse that covered the floor.

The huts were hollowed out inside to a depth of two feet or three feet below the ground-level. And thus, as Professor Peet says, 'what is actually found by the excavator is a hole filled with refuse and indistinguishable from the surrounding soil except by the colour of its contents. These holes are called *fondi di capanne* or foundations of huts. They are usually circular or elliptical, varying in diameter from two to seven or eight metres'. In the centre of this hole stood the hearth, probably built of clay, and round the hearth the excavator finds not only ashes and the burned bones of the meal, but also implements and pottery. These vary considerably in different regions ; which shows that, though the industries are generically alike all over the peninsula, there is a great deal of local individuality and original inventiveness. This is generally found to be the case anywhere in the world where people are living in small village communities, especially when the villages are isolated at considerable distances from one another.

Pottery, which is one of the most distinctive inventions of the Neolithic peoples everywhere, affords a good criterion of the artistic development of any particular branch of these peoples. Palaeolithic man had not learned to make pottery, but quite early in the New Stone Age this craft had been completely mastered. The potter's wheel was still unknown, but this was no disadvantage, for a broad survey of pottery made in various countries will show that the wheel, though a clever device, marks a step towards commercialization rather than an advance in art. Actually the handsomest and finest earthenware pottery, as distinct, of course, from faience or porcelain, has generally been made without the wheel. The most striking example of this fact, which is really a fact and not a paradox, is to be found in ancient Egypt, where the hand-made pottery of predynastic times was never equalled in later days. In Italy at this period the pottery is of a fairly high class, but it does not attain the extraordinary excellence of the contemporary products of Sicily. The most widely spread type of ware is a monochrome brown or black, coloured by the smoke of the open fire in which it was burned, and decorated with applied strips and ridges, or pitted with the finger or a pointed stick. Slip coatings were sometimes used to give a smoother surface to the half-purified clay; and the firing, though done without a kiln, was generally quite skilfully performed. In one district of the south, viz. near Matera, a very different ware has been found. This is incised with patterns in a style which somewhat recalls the Sicilian pottery of the same period, and may be related to it in some indirect fashion as a result either of trade or of immigration.

The implements are always of stone, for the use of metal was a discovery of the Orient which had not yet penetrated Europe. As with the pottery so with the stone implements and weapons, there is considerable diversity in the styles of manufacture. In some parts of the country the old Palaeolithic technique still survived, though enriched by some new and improved forms. In many other parts, however, there have been found finely polished axes and adzes, made of such rare and handsome materials as jadeite and nephrite. These remind us of the beautiful greenstone weapons of the New Zealand Maoris; and the accidental resemblance suggests the reflection that perhaps the life of the Maoris may provide a rather apt illustration of the grade of culture attained by the Italian aborigines. If that parallel is admissible it must be agreed that the grade is by no means low.

There is a considerable amount of evidence to suggest that the Neolithic Italians entertained far wider trade relations with the outside world than might have been expected. The use of obsidian both in Liguria and in Tuscany proves intercourse between the north and the Bay of Naples or the Lipari Islands. Some of the incised pottery of Matera and Molfetta is like enough to the contemporary Sicilian to suggest that it came from that island, unless it belonged to a tradition inherited from common ancestors. Certain painted pottery, also from Matera, so closely resembles Thessalian wares that it was probably imported from across the Adriatic. And, finally, the types of some peculiar weapons, such as the disk-shaped mace which is found in Saxony and Denmark, or the hammer-headed axe which was apparently invented near the site of Troy, justify the view that some connexion had already begun with the Danube and regions lying beyond the Alps.

CHAPTER 2

The Introduction of Metals

Metals came into use much later in Italy than in the Eastern Mediterranean. Dates for the first use of copper and bronze in Egypt, Spain, Hungary, Central Europe. The lake-dwellers and their connexions. Cemeteries of the Chalcolithic Age. Review of the weapons and implements found in these cemeteries. Complete absence of connexion with Sicily. The full Bronze Age begins with the Terremare. Characteristics of the Terremare and their inhabitants. Importance of these new arrivals as metallurgists and agriculturists. Commercial connexions, expecially with the Danube. No Mycenaean influence whatsoever. Rapid development of local metal-working and resultant exportation. Uniformity of Bronze Age culture in Italy. Review of improvements in standard of life since Neolithic time.

THE general adoption of the use of metals implies an immense advance in civilization owing to the mastery thereby acquired over every kind of material. This great step had been taken in the Eastern Mediterranean at a time when all Europe was still at the Neolithic stage. Copper was already known and used in Egypt even before the First Dynasty, and by the time of the great pyramid-builders it had become quite common. Early in the history of the Old Kingdom, moreover, the expedient had been adopted of alloying copper with tin, so as to lower the melting-point and also to produce a more durable substance.

Accordingly, bronze implements came into use in Egypt at a date which, by any reckoning, is at least as early as the middle of the third millennium B.C. The Egyptians obtained their copper chiefly from the peninsula of Sinai, while Cyprus naturally became the principal source of supply for Crete and the Levant. But the great demand for the new metals induced prospectors from Crete and from Anatolia to explore westwards by sea and by land. This process led to the opening up of Europe and the complete transformation of all European life.

In one direction the immediate effect of this exploring activity was to develop the copper mines in Spain; in another it led to the discovery of the mineral wealth of Hungary and Bohemia. From the close similarity of certain types found both in Spain and in Crete it is possible to obtain an approximate dating for the opening of the Spanish copper mines, which shows them to have been active at a time equivalent to the Egyptian Fourth Dynasty. The Danubian Copper Age in Hungary and Central Europe is probably a little later; but comparisons with the second city of Troy suggest that it had begun by the second half of the third millennium B.C.

The effect of all this activity upon Italy was for some time only indirect; for there is no evidence to show that the copper mines of Tuscany and Elba were used until much later. Copper daggers of the earliest Creto-Spanish types (Plate 1, no. 4) have indeed been discovered in several places, and because they have been found in a stanniferous region of Tuscany, it has been suggested that Aegean miners were already visiting the coasts of Italy in the second stage of the Early Minoan period. But such sporadic communications, if they ever took place, exercised little influence on the general development. The gradual change which substituted the Bronze Age for the Neolithic in Italy was not effected by the occasional inroads of wandering prospectors. It came rather as the irresistible consequence of a steady and consecutive process of penetration from the north. It was due to the swarming of new tribes from the other side of the Alps and to the inter-communication initiated by such movements.

The process begins with the appearance in the north-west corner of Italy of an entirely new people, overflowing apparently from the nearer parts of Switzerland. Like the Swiss lake-dwellers, they made their settlements in villages which they built on piles in shallow waters for purposes of defence. Gradually they extended their occupation over the whole chain of the Italian lakes from Maggiore to Garda, and even as far as the swampy regions about the Euganean hills in Venetia. No skeletal remains of them have been found, but, from their geographical origin and the character of their life, it seems quite likely that the lake-dwellers belonged to the type known as 'Alpine man', a short dark round-headed individual very unlike the representatives of the Mediterranean race. These Alpines cannot have been sufficiently numerous to affect the general distribution of the population, except locally in parts of Lombardy and Venetia, but their mere appearance on the stage is significant as a landmark in history. For it is the first example of that influx of northern aliens which becomes a regular process in the annals of Italy, repeating itself at short intervals throughout the next four thousand years.

The earliest lake-dwellings begin at the exact moment of transition from the Neolithic to the Copper and Bronze Age, a moment which in Italy may be placed a little before 2000 B.C. Some of them persist as late as 1000 B.C., after which they entirely disappear, and it is an unsolved problem what became of the inhabitants. The most probable view is that they became less amphibian in the process of time and were gradually absorbed by the surrounding Ibero-Ligurians. These lake-dwellers are perhaps more of a curiosity than a definite link in the chain of the country's progress, but their arrival synchronizes with the beginning of those trade-relations with Central Europe which became of such immense importance in the following centuries. In the lake-dwellings there

have been found numerous weapons and implements of cast bronze. These could not have been
manufactured in Switzerland, which did not
possess the metals, so it is clear that they must
have been derived, directly or indirectly, either
from Spain via the Riviera or else from Hungary
and Bohemia. The principal types show clearly
enough that the latter was the chief, though not
perhaps the only, source of origin. For by this
time there was already a flourishing metal industry on the Danube, and great commercial
routes were being opened up all over Central
Europe. The amber trade with the Baltic was
beginning, and may already have become quite
active; but the rarity of amber and the complete
absence of glass paste and other typical products
of trans-European trade in the settlements of the
lake-dwellers prove that they had not yet been
caught up into the full current of European commerce.

If we wish to form an estimate of the condition
of Italian life and industry at the very beginning
of the Bronze Age it is safer to study the cemeteries than the dwellings, because the chronology
of the latter is somewhat involved. There is quite
a risk, owing to the long life of the lake-dwellings,
and the difficulty of distinguishing the several
stages in them, that objects may be attributed to
2000 B.C. which are really five hundred years

later. Of the cemeteries Remedello, in the province of Brescia, is the largest and most famous;
others of less size have been found in the neighbourhood of Brescia and Modena, while sporadic
burials have been observed near Bologna, Ancona, Viterbo, and Benevento. From the evidence
obtained at places so widely separated as this it
becomes possible to review the Chalcolithic period
as it is seen over a considerable extent of country,
and to observe a good deal of local variation as
well as a strong resemblance of general character.

The first and principal conclusion that emerges
from such a review is that there has been no
revolutionary change; the Chalcolithic civilization
is simply a continuation of the Neolithic in an improved form. The lake-dwellers initiated no epoch-
making movement; their coming is rather an
incident than the immediate cause of a certain
general improvement in the standard of life. They
were, in short, far less important to Italian pre-
history than their successors of the Terremare,
whom I shall discuss when dealing with the full
Bronze Age.

At Remedello and similar sites copper or bronze
is still far from abundant. Many of the weapons
and implements are still made of stone, and some
of the Neolithic types such as the finely polished
celts still continue, as well as earlier and rougher
forms. But the stone arms and daggers of this

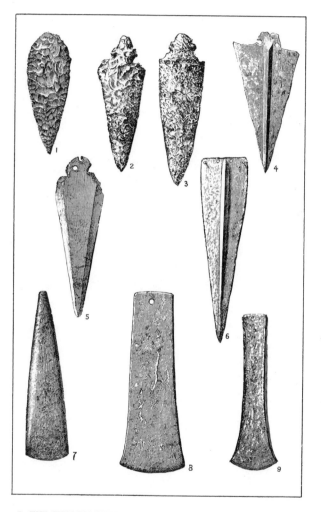

I. THE CHALCOLITHIC AGE.   STONE AND COPPER WEAPONS

period exhibit a new and very much improved technique. The flint-worker is no longer content with mere chipping; he has learned the much more difficult and skilful process of removing minute flakes from the edge by pressure. The actual implement used for this work was found in one grave at Remedello, viz. 'a small rounded core of flint in a handle of stag's horn' (Peet, p. 246). Flint daggers produced by this method are shown in my Plate 1, nos. 1–3, and it can be seen that they are exceedingly fine specimens. It is worth remarking, however, that the influence of metal prototypes is very perceptible. Flint-working and bronze-working were constantly acting and reacting upon one another at this time. If a stone dagger imitates the shape of a bronze dagger, yet the first copper axes are clearly copied from the stone celts. This may be seen from the flat axes so typical of the dawn of the Bronze Age shown in nos. 7, 8 of my Plate 1. But the most characteristic implement of the period is the copper dagger of such forms as are shown in my Plate 1, nos. 4, 5, 6. The latest stages of the Chalcolithic culture are represented by axes which are no longer smooth and flat but flanged at the edges like no. 9 in my Plate 1. These mark the beginning of the full Bronze Age, and may be dated nearer 1700 B.C. than 2000 B.C. One line of their subsequent evolution can be traced in Plate 2, nos. 1–3.

As I am concerned in this chapter only with the peninsula of Italy I shall not discuss the very interesting Chalcolithic civilization of Sicily, which will be briefly treated in my concluding chapter. It is curious to observe how little direct influence the one country seems to have exercised upon the other, but it must always be remembered that Southern Italy is virtually unexplored and may have surprises in store for any one who ventures on prophecy. We can only speak with any approach to certainty of the regions north of Rome Having dealt thus briefly with the earliest stages of the Bronze Age, I will now discuss the full Bronze Age, in which flint-working has disappeared and metal has come into universal use.

It is customary to associate the great development which began to take place about 1700 B.C. with a new and far more important immigration from beyond the Alps than that of the lake-dwellers. This fresh movement is from the north-east, and may be traced directly to the region of the Danube, which had now become the home of the most advanced European culture of the time. It synchronizes with the full Bronze Age of Central Europe, and brings Italy immediately into touch with all the commercial and industrial life that is beginning to develop there. The missionaries of the new civilization were the builders of the famous Terremare in the valley of the Po.

The word Terramara is an untranslatable piece of jargon, of which the derivatives are very difficult to manipulate in any language except Italian. It has been universally accepted as the technical term for a pile-dwelling on dry land, in a style unknown outside Italy, though it has certain general analogies on the Danube. As being semi-lake-dwellers the builders of the Terremare might be considered to belong to the same family as the real lake-dwellers, but if so it was at least a distinct branch, and we cannot safely hazard any guess as to their racial characteristics beyond saying that they were quite different from those of the Mediterranean race. Their settlements occupied the whole valley of the Po on both sides of the river, covering, therefore, a great part of the eastern area previously colonized by the lake-dwellers. Without necessarily subscribing to the popular theory that the people of the Terremare were the direct ancestors of the Latins, I find it so necessary to have a manageable title for them that I shall henceforward refer to them as the Proto-Italici.

They were a people of very strongly marked characteristics, differing in many respects from the Ibero-Ligurians, but most of all in their burial practice. Whereas the aborigines always retained the custom of burying their dead in the ground, the Proto-Italici cremated and deposited the ashes in large jars. Entire cemeteries of these cremation urns have been found outside their villages, built precisely like the villages themselves on piles which raised them some distance above the swampy ground. This contrast of burial rites serves, as will be seen, to distinguish the main currents of Italian population even as late as the Middle Iron Age. For the Ibero-Ligurians all over the peninsula maintained the practice of inhumation, whereas all the northern invaders down to the time of the Gauls belonged to cremating races.

The pile-built dwellings of the Proto-Italici have been so often described that I need not repeat the description. Only I feel obliged to register a note of warning against the usual theory that they were laid out on the same plan as Roman cities. Sergi's very telling criticisms on this point have never been quite satisfactorily answered, and in any case the argument that this system of planning is specifically Latin must completely collapse if it can be shown that the Romans themselves learned it from the Etruscans.

The importance of the Proto-Italici rests on two distinct grounds. In the first place they were highly skilled in metallurgy and in agriculture, so that their arrival must have had the effect of raising the whole material status of the country. And in the second place they evidently kept up a close connexion with their original home, situated in a densely populated and flourishing region

which contained the most thriving industrial
centres of the day. Thereby they made Italy the
terminus of branch lines connecting with the great
trunk routes of commerce over Europe. It is no
anachronism or exaggeration to use these terms
in speaking of the Bronze Age. One of the most
valuable results of comparative archaeology in the
last few years has been the demonstration that
from very early times a widespread system of
commercial intercourse existed all over the continent, from the Black Sea to the Atlantic and
from the Baltic to the Mediterranean. The second
millennium B.C. was the period of the opening up
and exploration of Europe, comparable to the
opening up of India and China by the western
nations after the fifteenth century A.D. Metals and
materials were the objects of search, and wherever
they were discovered it was likely that centres of
industry would spring up. Thus in particular the
copper of Hungary and the tin of Bohemia had
created a populous and flourishing series of stations
along the Danube, which became the principal
source of the Bronze-Age culture of Europe. The
Proto-Italici formed the liaison between the
Danube and Italy, which is the explanation of the
whole development of the Bronze Age in the
latter country.

For it must be plainly understood that the
Bronze-Age culture of Italy is in no sense depen-

dent upon the Mycenaean nor directly derived
from it. The analogy of Sicily must not mislead us.
Sicily was unquestionably in touch with the
Mycenaean world. Mycenaean vases and weapons
are found in Sicilian graves and the influence of
Aegean culture is unmistakeable. But the more we
study Sicily the more evident it becomes that the
whole development of Sicilian civilization is absolutely independent of Italy. Curiously enough, the
Straits of Messina seem to form a positive dividing
line. Right down to the full Iron Age there is a
complete absence of any interpenetration or intercourse between Sicily and Italy. In view of our
very slight knowledge of Southern Italy in the
Bronze Age it might be rash to exclude all possibility that Sicily may have influenced Calabria
and Apulia in some slight degree; but it is certain
that no such influence penetrated into Northern
or Central Italy; the civilization of the north and
centre at least is purely continental. Not so much
as a sherd of Mycenaean pottery has ever been
found between the Alps and the Gulf of Taranto.
And, if the bronze weapons and implements are
critically examined, it will be found that very few
resemble the Mycenaean, and these few are generally remote derivations modified by passage
through Danubian manufactories. Any part of its
Bronze Age culture which Italy did not derive from
the Danube may be ascribed to intercourse with

Spain, which was carried on by way of the Riviera, as is proved by the rock-drawings of Liguria.

A certain amount of maritime trade with Sardinia is also to be inferred, but it was not important enough to have any far-reaching consequences. Occasional objects of Aegean or Trojan origin, such as spiral-headed bronze pins, must have travelled by way of the Danube, as it is evident that there was no direct communication with Greece by sea. A few examples of amber, which could only have come from distant Jutland, show that the Proto-Italici derived some little advantage from the thriving trade between the Baltic and the Danube. But the very rarity of amber on Italian sites before the Iron Age suggests that the Terremare were a little off the main route, which can hardly have been deflected over the Brenner quite so early as this.

There is no doubt that the Proto-Italici were excellent bronze workers who not only imported but also manufactured many weapons and implements. The actual moulds for casting some of these have been discovered in their settlements. Certain forms of bronze daggers like those shown in Plate 2, nos. 5, 6, are recognized as specifically Italian, and these have been found on Bohemian sites of 1600 or 1500 B.C. Indeed, some entire Bohemian deposits of this date are so precisely like the Italian that it is difficult to say which owed most to the other. The bronze swords of the Terremare are quite different from all the Aegean types and may either have been imported or manufactured locally. One form shown as no. 4 in Plate 2 is merely an elongation of the native dagger like nos. 5, 6. From whatever source they derived their models it is quite evident that the Proto-Italici were producers as well as importers.

By about 1500 or 1400 B.C., then, the manufacturing ability of the Proto-Italici, coupled with their extensive commercial relations, had produced a uniform level of material culture over the whole of Italy. There is little or no difference between the bronze weapons and implements of the Terremare and those of Emilia, the Marche, and Venetia. In Latium, Tuscany, and Umbria not many Bronze Age sites have been excavated, but such as they are the products closely resemble those of the north. Even in Southern Italy, Terramara types of daggers and sickles have been found. Sicily, on the other hand, is wholly distinct, working out its own separate evolution with a considerable amount of help and suggestion from Mycenaean sources.

At the close of the Bronze Age, then, which may be placed about the thirteenth century B.C., Italy had become a partner sharing in most of the benefits of European commerce. She had also made a distinct position for herself as an indepen-

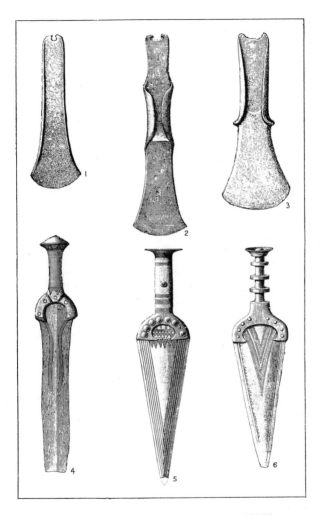

2. THE BRONZE AGE.   AXES, SWORD, DAGGERS

dent manufacturing country, if only on a small scale. The next chapter in the evolution of the country deals with the discovery and exploitation of its natural wealth, and the consequent movements and migrations of the population. Before passing on to this I may briefly summarize the changes and improvements which had taken place in Italian life as a whole since it was reviewed at the close of the last chapter, a period of about a thousand years.

The most notable change in the life of the people during the Bronze Age was the introduction of agriculture. It is doubtful whether Neolithic man in Italy was acquainted with any sort of cultivated grain. But in the lake-dwellings two kinds of wheat as well as millet appear at a quite early stage. The Proto-Italici were important to the country not only as metallurgists but also as agriculturists and farmers of stock. Flax, beans, and two types of wheat have been found in their dwellings, together with the stone handmills on which the grain was ground. Horses were known even to the lake-dwellers and were freely used by the Proto-Italici. Cart-wheels have been found both in the lake-dwellings and in the Terremare. Ploughs and hammers are depicted in rock-drawings of the same period in Liguria. Quite early in the Bronze Age two kinds of oxen appear, as well as sheep, goats, and pigs, while the farmyards of the Proto-Italici contained also fowls and ducks. In short we have a picture of a complete and almost modern farm-life. Dogs are already so familiar that three varieties are distinguished, the ancestor of them all being *Canis palustris*, doubtless a good woolly animal of a fair size.

Hunting of course was still a very necessary occupation, even more to provide food than to protect the farm; deer, wild boar, and bear being the principal game. There is very little evidence of fishing, but this may be due to the accidents of excavation. Canoes of the dug-out form were used, and have been found in good preservation, together with their paddles, in more than one of the peat-bogs. It is clear that the whole standard of life is very much higher than at the end of the Neolithic Age.

I have repeated in these first chapters several passages which occur in two of my papers written for *Antiquity* (March and June, 1928). These papers, entitled 'Forerunners of the Romans', were accompanied by some other illustrations which will be found a useful supplement.

CHAPTER 3

The Partition of the Country in 1000 B.C.

Invasions of Italy from north at end of Bronze Age. Resultant distribution of population about 1000 B.C. Picenes—Villanovans—Atestines—Comacines. Survivors of the aboriginal stocks—Apulia—Siculans—Etruscans.

THE period of transition from the Bronze to the Iron Age is still somewhat obscure, and it is only after an interval of two or three centuries that the archaeology begins to emerge in clear lines. In the course of the two hundred years preceding 1000 B.C. it seems probable that there were fresh invasions of Italy by tribes coming from beyond the Alps. Life was very active in the Danube region about that time, and the surplus population was going out in periodical swarms to the east and west of the Adriatic. The tradition of one such movement has come down to us in the story of the conquest of Greece by the Dorians. For Italy there is no tradition, but the archaeological facts may be best explained by supposing a similar invasion. There were sufficient lures to attract wandering hordes, who would be tempted by rich agricultural territories near the larger rivers, and mines of copper and even iron in the mountains. Probably when they started on their southward march the immigrants were ignorant of the iron to be found in Tuscany and Elba, but they must have known of the copper, for it had long been exported to Bohemia and Hungary. It is in these regions of Central Europe that the original home of the Iron Age invaders must be placed. They were of the same general stock as the people of the Terremare who had brought the knowledge and use of bronze into Italy, but they were not directly related to them. Their burial rite, however, was the same, for they burned their dead instead of burying them in the ground. It is this that immediately differentiates them from the aboriginal Neolithic population, which continued down to the later historic times to maintain its old custom of earth burial.

When the immigrations from the north were completed, about 1000 B.C., the map of Northern and Central Italy appeared as it is shown in Plate 3. A broad river of transalpine invaders had poured down from Istria and the passes of Tirol, submerging the original Neolithic inhabitants as far down the coast as Rimini, and then turning to flood the western half of the country down to the Alban hills. With the newcomers were amalgamated their kinsmen and predecessors of the Terremare movement, whose culture was so entirely absorbed as to lose all its own individuality. Consequently in the tenth century before Christ there are two and only two race-stocks to be considered, the cremating peoples west of the line

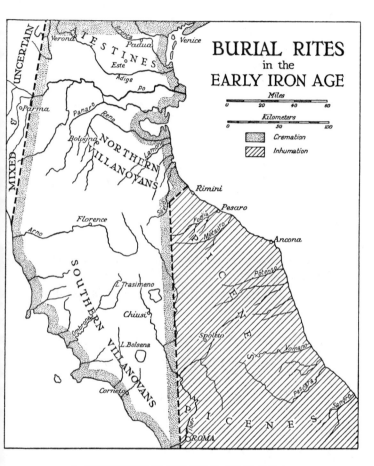

BURIAL RITES
in the
EARLY IRON AGE

Miles

0   20   40   60

Kilometers

0   50   100

Cremation

Inhumation

3. DISTRIBUTION OF PEOPLES ABOUT 1000 B.C.

from Rimini to Rome, and the burying peoples east and south of that line.

If it is asked what was the reason for the abrupt deflection of the invading stream at Rimini, and why it turned to the west instead of continuing down the east side of the Apennines, the answer seems clear. There is little doubt that what checked the invaders, and turned them aside from their natural course, was the resistance which they encountered from the native tribes in front of them. It would have been far more natural after reaching Bologna to continue down the trunk line of the modern railway and spread towards the Adriatic coast. There must have been some very strong reason which induced the immigrant hordes to cross the steep and deeply forested Apennines so as to descend into Tuscany. But when we come to study the Adriatic peoples, represented by the Picenes of the coast and the Samnites of the mountains, we shall find that for the next six or seven hundred years they were warriors of the fiercest kind. The Romans had every reason to know their prowess, and long before the Romans came into contact with them the character of the Picenes is attested by the contents of their tombs. Not a single man was buried without weapons, and these weapons represent a very formidable armoury. This explains why the vanguard of the invaders, avoiding the danger of battle or perhaps actually worsted in some preliminary encounter, preferred to settle in Tuscany and Latium rather than in Umbria and Picenum. The farthest southern point to which they penetrated was just beyond Rome and the Alban hills, where they made settlements as early as the twelfth or eleventh century B.C. Tuscany was occupied at virtually the same time, while the rearguard established itself at Bologna perhaps a little but not much later. The tribes that settled in these several provinces are so similar in all the details of their material civilization that it is convenient to group them under a single name. For reasons which will be given in the next chapter I have chosen to call them Villanovans. Those who planted themselves along the River Reno near Bologna may be called the *Northern* Villanovans, while the Iron Age inhabitants of Tuscany and northern Latium should be distinguished as *Southern* Villanovans. The two groups are closely related, but exhibit some slight variations of custom due to local circumstances and opportunity. The Villanovans are the most important of all the Iron Age peoples in Italy, except the Etruscans, who followed them in the ninth century, occupied the same area as the southern group, and built their own fortunes directly upon the foundations which had been laid for them by this fine barbaric people.

Besides the Villanovans two other important

groups of cremating tribes entered Italy at about
the same time. In the north-east a part of Venetia
was occupied by a very independent and original
people, whose power centred on Este and who
may therefore be christened Atestines. To the
west of these the lake region of Lombardy was
settled, though sparsely, by a fourth nation which
may be termed Comacine. Its earliest cemeteries
are found round the southern end of Lake Como,
which was probably reached by way of the Val di
Sole and the Valtellina. The Comacines never
developed any individuality of much importance;
but the Atestines soon rivalled the Bolognese in the
excellence of their manufactures, though their influence was almost confined to Venetia and the
adjoining Alpine country.

Besides these immigrant peoples, Villanovans,
Atestines, and Comacines, it is possible to identify
three groups of survivors from that old aboriginal
population which was vigorous enough to maintain its independence against the newcomers. The
largest and by far the most important of these is
the group named on my map as Picene; this includes Samnites and a certain number of Um-
brians, but is so homogeneous that it should
be called by a single name. These Picenes occupied the whole coast, together with the eastern
Apennines, from Rimini to Aufidena, while their
western outposts commanded the passes at Terni

and the road down the Tiber. A few of the same stock survived in Latium, and lived side by side with the Villanovans in the earliest community that inhabited the future site of Rome.

Immediately south of Picenum on the Adriatic coast is the large province of Apulia. Archaeological exploration of this region has been so slight that we know little of the inhabitants before 700 B.C., and even then can judge of their characteristics only by their pottery. From this, however, it is possible to form some conception of the character and the psychology of two very ancient tribes, which were known to classical writers as the Daunians and Peucetians.

On the west coast south of Rome exploration has also been very deficient; the small amount that can be learned as to Campania before the Greeks came to Cumae gives us little beyond the negative conclusion that the Villanovans never penetrated there. From Cumae to Cosenza is still an archaeological blank. But the veil has been partially lifted from the obscurity which shrouds the prehistory of the Bruttian peninsula, where it juts out to meet Sicily. Here in the last few years has been discovered a quite distinct native civilization belonging to the Siculi, who are mentioned by Polybius as inhabiting this very region, and who according to several ancient writers once occupied a large portion of Italy.

Finally, to these six nations, three of recent arrival, viz. Villanovans, Atestines, and Comacines, and three belonging to the aboriginal stock, viz. Picenes, Apulians, and Siculans, must be added a seventh. This is the nation of the Etruscans, who arrived later than any of the others, coming in from Asia Minor at the end of the ninth century. I have described them and their works in an earlier volume, and will here only say that they were the most important of all the factors which contributed to the civilization of Italy down to 400 B.C. In the succeeding chapters I shall consider the other six peoples in turn, and shall try to show how much each achieved in its own particular sphere, and how much each contributed to the permanent development of the country.

CHAPTER 4

The Northern Villanovans

Villanova. The Northern Villanovans. Tombs and ossuaries. General character of the First Benacci period. Dating.
Contents of graves. Villages—Dwellings—Dress and ornaments. Pottery making. Domestic animals. Hammered
metal-work. Transition to Second Benacci period. Increase
in use of iron. Extension of commerce. Use of ships. Bronze
ossuaries, situlae, and other vessels. Bologna becomes a
manufacturing centre. Metal-working dominant as an art.

THE term Villanovan does not of course occur
in ancient literature. We cannot ever know by
what name these early people called themselves.
But just as a single place like Hallstatt in Austria,
or La Tène in Switzerland, has given its name to
a phase of civilization spread widely over Europe,
so the insignificant Villanova has become the god-
parent of an epoch and of a group of nations.
Villanova itself is a hamlet five miles from Bologna,
at which in 1853 Count Giovanni Gozzadini, an
admirable archaeologist of the Victorian generation, found an ancient cemetery. It contained a
large series of earthenware jars, thickly concen-
trated in rows. Within each jar were a few human
bones incompletely consumed by fire, and around
it were several small pottery vases. In the bed of
ashes or resting upon it were various small objects
of bronze, iron, amber, glass, and bone, as well

as some bones of sheep, oxen, wild boar, and stag. This was the beginning of a series of excavations which have gone on for seventy years, as a result of which the Museo Civico of Bologna is now full of an enormous mass of material, which has been classified into three periods. The first two periods, with which this chapter deals, are called the First Benacci and Second Benacci. They cover a time which may be considered to run from some point in the eleventh century to nearly the end of the eighth. For present purposes I will treat them in general terms as equivalent to the three centuries 1000 B.C. to 700 B.C. Exactly where the dividing point between them comes is difficult to state in actual years, but provisionally we may put the end of the First period at 900 B.C. or perhaps a few years earlier.

The territory of the northern branch of the Villanovans though thickly settled was not very large. It extended from the River Reno to the Apennines, and from the River Panaro on the west to the Adriatic on the east. That is to say, it comprised the modern provinces of Bologna, Faenza, Forlì, and Ravenna. Cemeteries have been found all through this region, but the most extensive and important were in the suburbs and immediate surroundings of the city of Bologna. The essential feature in all the tombs is the ossuary, a tall jar of hand-made pottery, usually decorated with incised geometrical patterns and covered with an inverted bowl. It is of a peculiar and very characteristic form, like two cones placed one above another, with a pronounced waist of the style once fashionable in Pompadour dresses. Pictures of it are shown in Plate 4, nos. 3, 4. Sometimes the jar was laid in a plain round hole in the ground, sometimes it was enclosed by a covering of small stones, which in later stages might even become a rectangular cist. Among the ashes in the ossuary and around it were the small objects, implements, ornaments, and weapons, which were to accompany the dead person in the underworld. It is from a review of these that it is possible to fix the chronology, and to describe to some extent the life and character of the people.

No one who stands in front of the cases representing the First period in the museum at Bologna can fail to realize at once that he has passed far beyond the Bronze Age. Iron is indeed exceedingly rare, so rare that it did not occur at all in many hundreds of graves, but the whole feeling is that of the Early Iron Age, as a student knows it in any of the large collections belonging to other parts of Europe. The simple geometrical art is only a local variant of the school that extended all over Europe about 1000 B.C., and which is equally illustrated by Greece, the Balkans, Austria, or

Germany. The fibulae or safety-pins, which give a standard for serial dating in Europe, just as scarabs give it in Egypt, though unfortunately with less precision, are of Iron Age types. They are primitive, it is true, but it is a long process of evolution which separates them from the violin-bow form of the lake-dwellings. We can trace their pedigrees quite plainly, and almost count the number of generations that must separate them from the time of the Terremare. It is by such reasoning, which to an archaeologist is almost as good as a written document, that we arrive at an approximate dating for the First Benacci period. This is confirmed on the negative side by the total absence of any Bronze Age products, and is further checked by dead reckoning from the lower end, where we are aided by synchronisms with precisely dated Egyptian objects. By working backwards, and spacing out all the series which precede an inscribed jar dated by its Egyptian inscription to 700 B.C., it is possible to arrive at a fairly close approximation. So much may be said in regard to general method, without unduly wearying the reader with the technique of a specialist.

Many tombs in the First Benacci period were naturally quite poor, and often contained nothing but the ossuary with its covering bowl. In others there might be only one or two objects, a fibula or a razor, a head-pin, distaff, bracelet, fish-hook, or tweezer—always of course made of bronze. But from hundreds of deposits the total collection becomes quite large, and supplies sufficient material for a general picture. An occasional rich grave containing objects of remarkable excellence warns us not to place the standard too low, or to estimate the level of culture exclusively from the lower and middle classes. Aristocracy, and some measure of plutocracy, undoubtedly existed in the early Iron Age as well as before and after it.

The Villanovans of the tenth century were living in small but very well organized communities. In the neighbourhood of Bologna itself they had built four villages, some distance apart but within easy range of an afternoon's call. Underneath the streets and houses of the modern city have been discovered the foundations of these early dwellings, round huts very much like those used in Central Italy which are illustrated in my Frontispiece.

The clothing of the inhabitants was thick, made of the wool which was spun on the bronze distaffs of which specimens have been found. It was fastened with bronze safety-pins—for buttons had not yet been invented—which are prettily designed and of several varieties of pattern. The ancient Highland dress in Scotland will enable us to realize how a Villanovan looked when he went for a walk. During the First Benacci period the women must have been content with very few and simple ornaments ; even if they were the only wearers of the bronze armlets and safety-pins strung with amber, which are the most decorative objects of this time. Apart from these they had little but very plain finger-rings, hair-rings, and ear-rings. In the Second period, however, as will be seen, their protests had been heard, and there was a very notable increase in the number and variety of all sorts of feminine ornaments. This was only a just recognition of their activity in spinning, weaving, and the making of pottery, assuming that this latter task fell to the women as it generally does in early communities. The pottery, it may be said in passing, is all hand-made, and though the number of forms is very limited they are not without a certain grace. The only decoration of the pottery consists in a few simple geometrical designs, incised in the clay before burning.

As for the men of the First period it is known that they rode, for their handsome bronze bits ornamented with the bronze figurine of a horse at each end are among the best products of this early art. They kept dogs, and a bronze staff from one tomb is surmounted by a good model of a running dog. Of course they hunted, especially the wild boar and the stag, while by this time

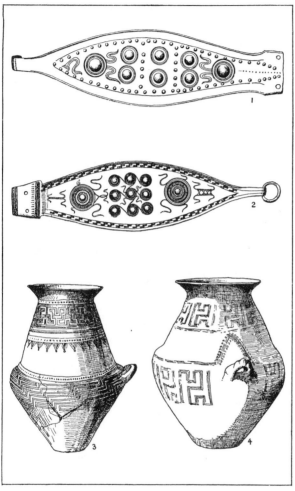

4. VILLANOVAN BRONZE GIRDLES AND POTTERY URNS

domestic animals such as sheep and oxen had been familiar for many centuries. Occasionally no doubt they had to go to war; swords, spears, and axes are found in the tombs, but these are not so frequent as to suggest that fighting was a constant occupation; the Villanovans were not primarily a nation of warriors like the Picenes. It is interesting to note that one of the swords is of a type well known in Central Europe and obviously imported into Italy; from the curving volutes of the hilt it is generally known as the 'antennae sword'.

Costly and elaborate articles are very rare in the First period, but when they occur they throw a wholly unexpected light on the artistic sense and technical ability of the tenth- and ninth-century Villanovans. By far the finest products of this period are belts hammered out of sheet copper, a process peculiarly distinctive of all this group of Danubian nations. In some cases the ornamentation is limited to rows of studs produced by hammering from the underside (Plate 4, no. 1). A more elaborate form of decoration, executed in the same technique of repoussé, is shown in no. 2 of Plate 4, in which engraving has been employed to fill out the details. Girdles of similar style have been found in Tuscany and in Venetia, but in both these provinces they belong to a slightly later period. Curiously enough the habit of wearing them seems to have gone out of fashion before the Second Benacci period, in which they hardly occur at all; but the manufacture was apparently kept up for purposes of export and trade.

The Second Benacci period at Bologna seems to evolve quite naturally and simply out of the First, without any abrupt transition. But there is a very great increase in wealth of all kinds, and in the variety of new materials. Manufactures must have developed apace, in order to enable the Villanovans to produce enough to exchange for all the numerous articles which they now obtained from abroad, as well as from other parts of Italy. Iron, which had been so rare before the ninth century, was now quite common. The nearest and most convenient source of it was Etruria, and, as the southern branch of the Villanovans was freely using iron at this time, it may be inferred that the mines of Tuscany had been opened and the resources of Elba were being exploited.

Glass-paste and amber, only occasionally found in the preceding century, were now abundant. As the amber had to come all the way across Europe from the Baltic this means that there was active commerce going on across the Alpine passes. Further evidence that the northern Villanovans kept up their connexion with Central Europe is provided by the types of the swords, still antennae-handled like those of the tenth century. It is probable that the numerous beads, made sometimes of glazed clay and sometimes of glass, arrived by the same routes, travelling up the Danube and then down through the Eastern Alps. Blue beads with small white eyes, or yellow beads with a blue centre, were favourite kinds and, like the amber, were often strung on safety-pins. Glass balls, three-quarters of an inch in diameter, made a very pretty and extraordinary modern-looking top to the bronze head-pins of the women; usually they were blue with spots or zigzags in bright yellow.

Commerce at this time, as I have said, proceeded mainly by land, but there is one curious piece of evidence which shows that the Bolognese of the eighth or ninth century were acquainted with ships. This is a rude drawing of a galley with mast and oars, accompanied by row-boats, incised on one of those half-moon blades which are generally called razors. The reverse side of this remarkable document shows the picture of an axe, precisely similar to the bronze axe-heads found in the tombs, hafted on to a long, curved handle of wood.

The technical ability, which in the First period had been confined to the production of one or two classes of objects such as the bronze belts, was now exercised in a much more varied field. With the increase of luxury many objects of ritual or of daily life assumed artistic forms. This change appears first in the production of large ossuaries of bronze, made in a shape derived from that of the pottery ossuary but more delicate in outline and fitted with a pedestal. In Plate 5, nos. 5 and 6, I show two of these together with an early example of the situla or bronze bucket (no. 4) for which Bologna no less than Este was to become famous in future years. It has a lid with a handle to it formed in the shape of two ducks' bills. On some of the bronze work of this time the influence of Etruscan models is quite perceptible, which shows that the date must be eighth century. Thus there is one of these food-trays (no. 1), of which the finest examples have been found at Veii and Caere, and some beautiful fluted bowls (e.g. no. 2) that might have come from Caere itself. But it is not necessary to regard any of these as actual imports, the technique of manufacture is purely Villanovan. If the Etruscans furnished some models and suggestions to the Bolognese it is quite arguable that they received as good as they gave. I have suggested, for instance, that the girdles found at Corneto and Vetralla may very probably be of Bolognese manufacture. At Vetulonia, again, there are bronze water-vessels modelled on the same lines as the ossuaries illustrated in Plate 5, nos. 5, 6. To those who might reason that the series should be read in the inverse direction, and that all the bronze vessels in question, whether in Etruria or Bologna, are of Etruscan origin, I should reply that the process of working in hand-hammered sheets is not Etruscan, and that the more primitive forms are precisely those which are derived from the definitely Villanovan ossuary. It is certainly a fact, however, which must not be ignored, whatever interpretation may be placed upon it, that there is a close resemblance between much of the bronze work of the Second Benacci at Bologna and that which is found in the tombs of Etruscan Vetulonia. Here is a field for much study, and I freely admit the possibility of differences in interpretation. But one rule must be borne in mind whenever an interpretation is suggested. No primitive man any more than any modern man is willing to trade something for nothing. Supposing that the Villanovans of the north received anything from the Etruscans they must have given something in exchange. If it was not metal work that they gave, what can it have been?

Bologna, then, in the eighth century was successfully establishing herself in the position which she was to hold for another four hundred years as the Birmingham of Italy, the centre of an extensive export trade in bronze and iron work of all kinds. We can trace many Bolognese objects in the neighbouring Venetia, in spite of the fact that Este possessed its own very important and inde-

5. VILLANOVAN WORK IN HAMMERED BRONZE

pendent manufactories. The half-moon blades called razors were sent far and wide over Italy. Wavy-bladed knives, sometimes of iron but more often of bronze, were turned out in large numbers; a peculiar form of knife, shaped like a painter's palette knife, is not uncommon. Bronze axes were numerous in the graves, but the comparative rarity of other weapons is rather curious. No spears were found, and only three bronze swords, one of which is of the imported antennae type, while the two others are too broken to be recognizable. For the women, and perhaps also for the men, were made numerous fibulae of iron and bronze, quite handsome armlets of bronze and also of iron, as well as head-pins, finger-rings, and hair-rings. Women's implements such as distaffs and spindles were finely finished, and could not be better made in modern days.

The working of metal was such a dominant interest at Bologna that it came to be expected that every useful thing should be made of bronze or iron. Even the potters were affected by the universal fashion, so that earthenware food-stands or censers, copying a model that was probably Etruscan, were made with open-work pedestals and even sometimes hung with little chains moulded out of clay. In some other respects, too, the potters of this time were becoming quite sophisticated and beginning to adopt foreign ideas; fancy shapes appear sporadically; there are one or two instances of the curious trick of producing patterns by inserting a strip of tin. Paint also is now used occasionally, though rarely, in the decoration of pots. Evidently the manufacturers of all classes were wide awake to every suggestion that came in from abroad, and the world at the time was full of new ideas, of which a good many came through to Bologna.

CHAPTER 5

The Southern Villanovans

Dwelling-houses. Models of houses used as ossuaries. Contrast between Villanovan and Etruscan plan of house. Minor differences of burial custom and tomb-furniture. Etruria affected by foreign influence earlier than Bologna. The First Benacci period at Selciatello. The Second Benacci cemeteries of Corneto. Bronze helmets and girdles. Fusion between the latest Villanovan and earliest Etruscan.

THE earliest settlements of the southern Villanovans must probably be dated as early as the eleventh or twelfth century B.C. They were made in the mountainous Etrurian district of Tolfa and at a whole series of stations in the Alban hills. Contemporary, or almost contemporary, with these are the first graves in the fraction of ancient cemetery excavated by Boni in the Forum at Rome, where the newly arrived Villanovans seem to have lived quite peaceably and amalgamated with the native population.

The general manner of life was much the same in Etruria or Latium as that which has been observed among the Northern Villanovans. We are enabled to understand the precise character of the dwelling-houses from models which have been found in the tombs. My frontispiece, which shows the house of a prehistoric Roman some

6*a*. HUT-URN FROM CASTEL GANDOLFO

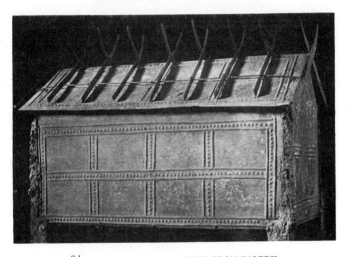

6*b*. BRONZE MODEL OF HOUSE FROM FALERII

three centuries before the time of Romulus, is taken from an example actually found in a grave in the Forum. Similar models have been found on several sites in Etruria, as well as at Grotta-ferrata and Castel Gandolfo. Some of the most interesting may be seen in the Museo Preistorico at Rome, and others in the Vatican 'Museo Etrusco'. These houses were evidently built of wattle and daub, with a roof of beams sometimes carved with decorative forms. The figure of a bird is occasionally used as the finial of a beam. Solid doors fastened with a bronze bar secured the entrance, and the smoke-hole in the roof formed quite an architectural feature. One hut-urn from Castel Gandolfo illustrated in Plate 6 *a*, has an external porch of wooden columns.

There is evidence that this style of dwelling persisted for several centuries, so that we may fairly infer that the Rome of Romulus was composed of round houses looking like these huts. The oblong plan for buildings seems to have been an Etruscan invention; the model of one of the earliest Etruscan houses is shown by a bronze ossuary from Falerii illustrated in Plate 6 *b*. It is well known that Etruscan temples were built down to the fourth century B.C. of unburned brick with beams and roofing of wood. Consequently, as it is not likely that the dwellings of the gods were inferior to those of the ordinary citizen, the Rome which was burned by the Gauls must have been still a town of mud-brick houses. From allusions in classical writers it appears that wooden roofs were common as late as the third century, and that fires were frequent.

There is no ready-made division into two periods for the three centuries 1000 B.C. to 700 B.C. in Etruria and northern Latium such as that which has been described in the last chapter. At the two extremes we can observe on the one hand the exceedingly primitive tone of the eleventh and tenth centuries, and on the other the remarkably advanced civilization of the eighth, when the influence of the Etruscans begins to be strongly felt. Sites, however, like pre-Etruscan Vetulonia or early Corneto cover the entire range of time, and enable us to trace the gradual development of the Villanovans, from their first rather barbaric beginnings down to the time when they began to learn better standards from the Etruscans.

Certain minor differences in burial custom can be observed between the southern and the northern branches of the Villanovans. South of the Tiber, that is to say in Latium, the standardized ossuary invariably employed at Bologna was never used; the cremated ashes were usually placed in some form of hut-urn, which was enclosed with all the other tomb-furniture in an immense jar. North of the Tiber, in Etruria, the Bolognese type of ossuary was usual but not invariable, as on some sites ordinary household jars were used instead. In Etruria the ossuary was often covered with a helmet instead of a bowl, and was enclosed in a cylindrical box of stone with a neatly-fitting lid.

A great deal of the tomb furniture is quite different in the two regions, respectively north and south of the Apennines, and especially the pottery. All Latian pottery has a strong local character. It belongs to a tradition which is very old, and is diffused with a certain amount of provincial varia- tion not only over Campania but even farther south. In fact the Latians seem to occupy in regard to culture the precise position which their geographical position would lead us to expect. A few miles south of the Tiber is the meeting- point of the Villanovan and aboriginal Italian; the civilization which results from their fusion retains characteristics derived from each ancestor.

In Etruria, on the other hand, the preceding Italian stock was completely absorbed, so that from the Arno to the Tiber it became purely Villanovan. There are a good many differences however, between Bologna and Etruria, due to the coastal position of the latter province, which made it more accessible to foreign influences coming in by sea. It is clear that, even before the coloniza- tion by the Etruscans, foreigners often touched, and occasionally traded, at various points on the coast

of the Tyrrhene sea, and their presence can be
detected by the contents of the tombs. Thus the
Etruscan settlement at Vetulonia is preceded by
a series of burials in which numerous objects
occurred which were quite unknown in any previous stage. Scarabs of amber, and Egyptian
glazed scarabs, a disk of gold ornamented with
geometrical designs, a sword-sheath engraved
with a hunting scene, silver fibulae and silver
bracelets, are definite proofs of the presence or
the visits of traders from the Aegean. This is at a
stage which I should date as near the end of the
ninth century, or perhaps early in the eighth.
At Corneto a cemetery of the same date furnishes
an indubitable instance of the actual presence of
a small colony of foreigners, who used a different
style of burial from their neighbours and brought
in the earliest geometrical pottery, which is derived directly or indirectly from the contemporary
geometric wares of Greece.

The steps by which these outside influences
penetrated into Etruria can be traced at Corneto
in four cemeteries which follow an exact serial
progression. The earliest of these, Selciatello, is
equivalent to pure First Benacci; the next, Poggio
dell' Impiccato is partly First and partly Second
Benacci; the third, Sopra-Selciatello, is full Second
Benacci; and the last, Monterozzi, is rather late
Second Benacci.

The picture presented by the Selciatello cemetery is very similar in its general outlines to that
of the First Benacci period at Bologna. All the
ossuaries except two were of the standard type
used at Bologna, and they were usually covered in
the same way with inverted bowls, though in five
cases the pottery model of a helmet was substituted for the bowl. Iron occurs, but is uncommon; amber and glass appear, but only sparsely;
and the fibulae are often of the most archaic
forms. The occurrence of gold is noteworthy,
though it is only in the form of small pieces of
plain sheet or plain wire, because gold was unknown in Bologna as early as this. A fine bronze
sword of an Aegean type is also unlike any model
known at this date north of the Apennines. The
pottery of Selciatello, however, was purely native
Italian, without any trace of foreign influence.

A very marked advance on anything seen at
Selciatello is shown by the two Second Benacci
cemeteries. At Poggio dell' Impiccato and Sopra-
Selciatello there is a sudden flowering of the finest
possible work in bronze. Two tombs on the first-
named site produced the helmets shown in Plate 7
and Plate 8, nos. 1 and 2. These illustrate the
high-water mark of metal-working among the
Southern Villanovans. It is still purely native,
and unaffected by foreign inspiration, at the
time of the ninth or early eighth century. From

whatever source the forms of the helmets may be derived the technique of the manufacture is absolutely Villanovan, and the decoration is of the purest geometric style, without any of that luxuriance of floral and zoomorphic design which came in with the very first appearance of the Etruscans. To appreciate this it is only necessary to contrast the contents of these tombs with the earliest Etruscan tombs of Vetulonia, where Oriental motives occur from the very beginning.

The closest parallel to the style of these helmets is to be found in the bronze girdles of Bologna, and there is little to choose between the two in respect of quality. In the Monterozzi cemetery was actually found a bronze girdle, which may be either a direct importation from Bologna or a local imitation. It is possible to suppose either that skilled craftsmen, like the Comacine masters in Lombard days, travelled to and fro across the Apennines, or that the Southern Villanovans were simply practising an art which they had learned in their original homes. The complete absence of any work of this kind during the First period in Etruria rather tells in favour of the first hypothesis.

The crested helmet shown in Plate 7 covered a typical Villanovan ossuary, made of pottery and ornamented with geometrical designs in a style superior to anything previously seen on these jars. The careful division of the field into panels is to be

7. POTTERY URN COVERED WITH BRONZE HELMET, CORNETO

remarked, and the use of the swastika; two features which can be matched, however, on a hut-urn of the preceding period at Selciatello. This helmet is ornamented with a double row of dots in repoussé work, while a similar double line runs round the edge of the crest. Of a quite different type are the cap-shaped helmets shown in Plate 8, nos. 1, 2. Such a motive as the schematically drawn human face with eyes, nose, and mouth, is quite unknown on any work of the time ; but the lines of dots and concentric circles, as well as the birds' heads, are quite in the same character as the decoration of Bolognese girdles.

In the latest of the four cemeteries at Corneto, called Monterozzi, may be seen the moment of fusion between the original Villanovan and the newly-arrived Etruscan in which neither has yet ousted the other. It is a most interesting stage of transition, to be dated to the early eighth century. Villanovan helmets and girdles and Villanovan ossuaries, imitating the standard form in bronze instead of pottery, may be seen side by side with Hallstatt swords, Etruscan candelabra, and bronze water-bottles derived through a series of copyists from an old Egyptian form (Plate 8, nos. 3–6). One of the earliest examples of Etruscan jewellery, a gold fibula ornamented in filigree and granulation, was found in the same tomb with an in-dubitably Villanovan bronze ossuary. This is the

last generation in which the genuine Villanovan
civilization can be seen still surviving in its typical
aspects; for in the seventh century it was amalgamated with the Etruscan and lost all its distinctive character.

It must surely be admitted that the Villanovan
had achieved a high standard. With very little
assistance or inspiration from outside he had
attained to a degree of barbaric culture which
entitles him to rank as high as any of the peoples
of the geometric age in Europe. It was inevitable
that Villanovanism should be forced to yield to
the superior organizing force and superior equipment of the Etruscans. No one can say what such
a virile and original race might have produced
had it been left independent. Under Etruscan
domination, however, it was not obliterated; on
the contrary we may detect in the Villanovans the
real backbone of the Etruscan nation. Like the
Saxons in England they formed the permanent
and enduring fabric of the nation, which changed
its name but not its essential character.

8. HELMETS AND VESSELS OF BRONZE, CORNETO

CHAPTER 6

Bologna in the Arnoaldi Period

Contrast between Bologna and Etruria from 700 to 500 B.C.
These centuries mark the zenith of Etruscan achievement.
But Bologna was unaffected by new movements. The Arno-
aldi period was a time of commercial prosperity but of no
artistic development. Establishment of Etruscan colony of
Felsina. The Etruscans absorb the Villanovans of Bologna.
Value of this provincial civilization of the Etruscans.

IF we now compare the art-history of Bologna
from 700 to 500 B.C. with that of Etruria the
contrast is very startling. South of the Apennines
these two centuries mark the zenith of Etruscan
achievement. The exquisite gold-work of Vetulonia has reached its highest point of excellence
by the middle of the seventh century. All the
wealth of jewellery, bronzes, carved ivories, and
silver bowls found in the magnificent tombs of
Caere and Praeneste belongs to the first half of the
seventh century. Then by 600 B.C. the orientalizing period of Etruscan art is beginning to pass, and
to make room for a phase in which the purely
Greek predominates. In the course of the sixth
century the spread of Etruscan power into Campania and Umbria on the one side, and the trade
between Tarentum and Apulia on the other, filled
all the accessible parts of Central and Southern

Italy with the finest art products of the contemporary world.

But, while this ferment of new life and civilization was stirring in all the regions of the south and centre, the country north of the Apennines remained isolated and unaffected. Bologna behind her mountains lived on tranquilly as if nothing unusual was happening. Two or three tiny pieces of jewellery are the only tangible proof of intercourse with the Etruscans about 700 B.C.; one black figured vase has been found in a sporadic burial of about 550 B.C.; except for these it might almost have seemed that the very existence of Greeks or Etruscans was unknown in Bologna before the closing years of the sixth century. It is an extraordinary and almost unnatural instance of isolation, which entailed every possible disadvantage to the mental health and progress of the people so isolated.

It must not be supposed of course that industry or commerce stagnated. There is another side to the picture, and it cannot be denied that the Arnoaldi period at Bologna witnessed a notable increase in material prosperity and wealth of all kinds. Iron has become so common that it is used with the utmost prodigality, huge iron pike-heads over a foot long are produced in abundance. Iron axes are no less frequent, and there are many iron swords. Chariots were now used for the first time—this at least was one thing learned from the Etruscans—and iron was used for the chariot wheels. Glass and amber also became very abundant.

But there is not a single piece of work in any branch which can arouse the slightest thrill of admiration. The free inventive spirit of the earlier periods seems to be dead. There is a uniform disheartening level of high-class factory work. Bologna has become a manufacturing centre, with no soul for anything but manufacture; not interested in learning anything from all the new influences with which she is surrounded, except a few mechanical tricks for time-saving.

The shelves of the Museo Civico are full of rows on rows of ribbed cists and situlae of bronze, all repeating the same forms with a wearisome iteration, and all embossed with the same tiresome rows of dots which were supposed to be decorative. There are few new shapes in the bronze work, and these few are not interesting. The history of the pottery is typical and characteristic. In the Benacci periods the decoration of the pottery had been done by hand, the patterns were incised with a point on the wet clay before it was baked; but in the Arnoaldi period the designs were produced mechanically by the employment of wooden stamps. Some of the new ideas prevalent throughout the surrounding world could not be wholly excluded, and accordingly we see that the simple old schemes of geometric patterns have been discarded. In their place there are schematically drawn figures of men or animals, and the inevitable water-birds, sometimes realistically executed but often quite carelessly rendered. The dignified old Villanovan ossuary has often been degraded into almost unrecognizable travesties inexcusably ugly in form.

In every branch the same reign of bad taste can be seen. Presumably the *art nouveau* of the Arnoaldi period achieved local popularity, and that amount of provincial fame which is proper to all *art nouveau*. But it can have had little success in the rest of Italy, for it is not found outside the boundaries of the northern Villanovan provinces. The mechanical ability of the workmen, however, was real and undeniable; and it was no doubt sufficiently recognized to enable Bologna to retain the northern market for situlae, and other trade articles which had been manufactured there for generations.

During the last years of the sixth century the Etruscans initiated their new policy of planting colonies north of the Apennines. One of the first, and always the most important, of these was Felsina, which they founded on a part of the space occupied by medieval and modern Bologna.

The Etruscan cemetery of Felsina was on a different site from the Villanovan, separated from it by a wide interval of empty ground as well as by a boundary ditch. Consequently there is no possibility of confusing the one with the other. It is a striking fact, therefore, when we find, not only that the two communities lived entirely apart, but also that they took hardly any interest in each other's activities. Not a single Etruscan article of this period has been found buried in a Villanovan grave, nor any Villanovan article in an Etruscan grave. There could be little doubt, however, which of the two rivals would survive; so that not long after the beginning of the fifth century Villanovanism practically died out, while the provincial Etruscan capital prospered until it was destroyed by the Gaulish invasion of about 400 B.C.

The local civilization of the Etruscans of Felsina is of considerable value and interest during the hundred years through which it lasted. It was always somewhat provincial in character, but it was far superior to the decadent Villanovan and exercised a considerable influence over the northern parts of Italy. We shall see that the Comacines of the lakes owed a good deal in the fifth century to the Etruscans, which means the transapennine colonies of which Felsina was the chief. More important in its consequences was the occasional inspiration which Felsina supplied to the vigorous and independent art of Venetia described in my next chapter. The famous situla of the Certosa of Bologna, dating from almost exactly the year 500 B.C., was one of the finest products of this provincial Etruscan art. I have described it elsewhere, and will here only say that it gives a series of delightful pictures of the country life of the day, together with all the games and accessories of a funeral procession. This was the original model from which the Benvenuti situla was copied, and the Benvenuti situla itself became the parent of a whole series of situlae which penetrated into the Alpine valleys from the Brenner to Lower Austria and have been found almost as far north as the Danube.

CHAPTER 7

Este and the Atestines

Geographical conditions of Este. Change in course of the Adige. Atestine civilization constantly developing from 900 to 500 B.C. Similarity to Bologna of the Second Benacci period. Este and Bologna distinct as centres of metal-working. Question of priority in invention of situlae and girdles. Peculiar effect of metal industry on styles of pottery. Indirect commerce with Mediterranean. New art developed about 500 B.C. The figured bronzes. The Benvenuti situla. Deterioration in fourth century.

NEXT in importance to the Villanovans as a factor in the development of the Early Iron Age were the Atestines. Their civilization, however, developed a little later and only reached its zenith during those very years when Villanovanism was slowly dying at Bologna. To those who think in terms of modern geography it will seem strange that so remote and isolated a spot as Este should have been the centre for many centuries of a very vivid life and active commerce. But the explanation may be found in the remarkable change which has taken place in the whole condition of the local landscape. All those miles of flourishing orchards and fields which now surround the little market town actually mask a long line of sand-dunes, which once fringed a river-bed and were only reclaimed for cultivation in the

Middle Ages. The Adige, which now flows nine miles to the south, used to wash the very walls of Este. A writer of the fifteenth century describes from his own observation a six-arched Roman bridge then spanning the old bed of the stream close to one of the ancient gates, and many traces have been found of Roman dykes and hydraulic works. It was only in A. D. 589 that, as a consequence of an extraordinary flood, the river found itself a new bed, leaving Este stranded far inland. Up to that date it had been in the position of a possible sea-port, on a river which was perhaps too turbulent and dangerous for much traffic, but offered much the same outlook as the later ports of Adria and Spina on the Adriatic. In the sand-dunes along the sides of the old river-channel have been found most of the cemeteries from which we derive our knowledge of the vanished history.

Evidence for any First period corresponding to the First Benacci period of Bologna is so slight that it may be disregarded for purposes of general treatment. It is by no means certain that the Atestines even founded their settlement before the end of the tenth century; in any case the earliest cemeteries yet discovered hardly begin before 900 B. C. The succeeding four hundred years mark a constant development, which reaches its highest point about 500 B. C., and is followed by a steady decline after the middle of the fifth century.

During the Second Benacci period the life of Este was exceedingly similar to that of Bologna. Not only the burial rites but the actual details of tomb construction were identical in the two places, and in many respects the contents of the graves are almost interchangeable during the ninth and eighth centuries. There are the same types of weapons and implements, the same varieties of fibulae, bracelets, necklaces, and other ornaments. At first sight it seems almost as if we were dealing with only one people. But a more detailed analysis brings out the differences, showing that there are some Atestine objects which do not occur at all in Bologna, while there are many things at Bologna which remained unknown in Este.

As centres of metal-working Este and Bologna are quite distinct, even though many of the small objects are identical. From the very beginning of the ninth century Este was producing large vessels in hammered bronze, receptacles in metal which enclosed the ossuary and objects placed with it in the same way as the huge pottery jars used in Latium. And no less early was the production of bronze situlae intended to be used as ossuaries. It has been much debated whether Este or Bologna originated the situla, or rather which of the two first converted the ordinary household bucket into an object of beauty and ceremonial use (Plate 9, nos. 1 and 2). On the one hand, the very archaic cemetery of San Vitale at Bologna contained fragments of situlae ; on the other, the earliest Second Benacci grave at Este produced an exceptionaHy fine example. If the chronology can be adjusted my own inclination is to give the priority of invention to the Atestines, if only on the ground that from the very first they showed a preference for using metal ossuaries rather than pottery, and did not adopt the regular Villanovan urn as their standard of form. In any case, the style of the situlae manufactured at the two places is always different; the Bolognese types usually have swing-handles; those of Este have seldom any handles at all, and if they have them the handles are fixed.

A similar question of relative priority comes up in regard to the decorated bronze girdles. A magnificent specimen from Este, attributable to the eighth century, is so like one at Bologna that the two might have been produced by the same hand. Here I am inclined to think that Bologna was first in the field, for the manufacture of bronze belts was characteristic of the First rather than of the Second period among the Northern Villanovans; and it is quite likely, as was said in the fourth chapter, that Bologna exported these masterpieces of her coppersmiths into Venetia as well as into Etruria.

Nevertheless, the independent origin of metal-

9. BRONZE SITULAE AND STUDDED POTTERY.　ESTE

working at Este seems to be clear, and we must suppose that the Atestines brought their knowledge and expertness in this craft from the Danube, where it had long been practised. The process used in the making of the large vessels has already been described; sheets of metal were hammered by hand, and decorated, if so required, with ornaments in repoussé, after which they were folded over and fastened with rows of large rivets arranged so as to make a decorative pattern. That commercial relations were kept up with Central Europe is shown by the presence of Hallstatt swords in several ninth-century tombs, as well as by the constant use of amber.

A striking result of the dominance of metal-working in Atestine life is seen in the manufacture of the pottery. Throughout the eighth and seventh centuries there seems to have been a constant effort to produce a pottery substitute for the bronze ossuary, and to make it appear as like metal as possible. This idea originated a very curious hybrid style. Vessels of lustrous black pottery were made in the situla shape and studded all over with large-headed bronze nails in evident imitation of repoussé work. The nails were embedded in the clay before firing, and if the process was successful the result was extraordinarily effective and might almost deceive the eye. In Plate 9, nos. 3–5, I show three examples of this work, which continued as a fashion down to about 500 B.C., when it was discarded in favour of the more legitimate production of handsome coloured wares.

From 900 to 500 B.C., then, Este was steadily and strongly developing her local culture, at first in close intercourse with Bologna, but in the latter part of the period indebted for little or nothing to her neighbour on the south of the Po. Just at the close of the sixth century, but not earlier, there are some indications of a commerce, which was probably indirect, with the Mediterranean. A tomb of only a few years before 500 B.C. contains a necklace with bone pendants carved into schematic figures which may represent a goddess. These have been claimed to be of Oriental origin, and, if so, they are the first examples in Venetia of a trade which no doubt passed through the hands of the Etruscans. For there is no evidence whatsoever of any direct overseas traffic at this date; the possibilities of Este as a seaport had not yet been realized by the carriers of merchandise from the Aegean, and not a sherd of Greek pottery has been found in Venetia before the fifth century.

The first half of the fifth century marks the highest point of Atestine achievement, and the best products of this generation were the figured situlae and figured bronze girdles. Up to the year 500 B.C. all the decoration on Atestine bronze work had been exceedingly simple. It was limited to a very primitive scheme of bosses and circles, arranged in rows according to the canons of that geometric school which had so long been traditional in Northern Italy no less than in Central Europe. We have seen in Chapter V how this school was transformed in the central provinces by the new ideas introduced by the Etruscans. The same thing happened in Venetia, only the change came two hundred years later than in Etruria. This was because the first close contact of the Atestines with the Etruscans only began when the latter founded their colony at Bologna. Certainly it could not be the result of mere accident that almost exactly in the very year 500 B. C. all the motives in Atestine art are suddenly changed, so that a wholly new school of design appears for the first time at that precise date. In tombs of which one can be dated very closely to the year 500, and others to the succeeding fifty years, there suddenly appears a whole series of figured bronzes in which plants, animals, and men are treated with a freedom and a skilled certainty of touch that rivals the work of Ionic Greeks. Birds and deer, cattle and horses, are represented with a perfect mastery and surety which seem almost incredible when we realize how short a time must have sufficed for the formation of this new school. But internal evidence leaves no doubt that it really is a native school and not a mere collection of imports; very few if any of these pieces were brought in from outside. The explanation of this sudden and unexpected development is furnished by a study of the famous Certosa situla of Bologna. This, as Ducati has convincingly shown, depicts an Etruscan funeral procession, in which the burial-urn is taken to its resting-place, accompanied by the attendants who are to carry out the sacrifice, and by the ox and sheep that are to be the victims. A detachment of soldiers of the several arms escorts the *cortège*, and a separate series of scenes describes the daily life of the Etruscans, with its ploughing and hunting, its music and games.

And if this Certosa situla is compared with the most famous piece of bronze work ever produced at Este, viz. the Benvenuti situla, which is about twenty years later in date, it becomes immediately evident that the Atestine work is a deliberate imitation of the Bolognese. I reproduce some of the principal scenes in Plate 10, nos. 3–5, omitting the boxing-match and some minor details. Every phase in the Benvenuti situla has its more or less close prototype in the other. It is not, indeed, a copy, but it is a direct translation, though a free translation. In the Benvenuti example the purpose is no longer to represent a funeral : the preparations for the burial and sacrifice are omitted : only the accessory scenes of country life and sports are chosen for treatment.

But the soldiers are there just because they were in the Etruscan model; for the same reason the boxing-match is there, the ravens, and, most unmistakable of all, the mythical animals inseparable from the Etruscan cult. There can be no possible doubt as to the parentage of the Benvenuti bronze work, but it is very interesting to see the variations on the original theme produced by the local artist. And it is also worth while to note how far superior this Atestine example is to a situla called the Arnoaldi, which was made at Bologna fifty years later. Bolognese art degenerated more quickly even than Atestine in the fifth century.

There was a brilliant period of fifty years during which very beautiful figured situlae were produced at Este under the new inspiration. No more translations of whole scenes occur, but there are charming decorative friezes of birds or animals such as are shown in my Plate 10, nos. 1 and 2. The ultimate derivation of this style is really Oriental: the Etruscans had borrowed it from the Cypriots, and by a curious roundabout route the orientalism of the seventh century has come to affect Venetia in the fifth.

The high level of art which has just been described was not maintained for more than two or three generations; the situlae of the fourth century show a great deterioration in style, though the technical execution is as perfect as ever. By

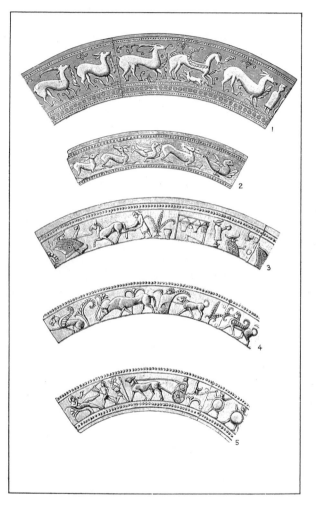

10. SCENES FROM BRONZE SITULAE.　ESTE

this time the craftsmen of Este had become completely commercialized: they were content to work as mere copyists on a stale repertoire of thrice-borrowed orientalizing motives combined without taste or discrimination. They had a market among the transalpine barbarians, with whom fourth-hand travesties of the Certosa masterpiece were very popular. As a commentary on misplaced enthusiasm it need only be mentioned in passing that these grotesque productions have sometimes been treated as if they were an indigenous 'Illyrian' art. South of the Po, of course, they were never even asked for; the beautiful works of Greeks and Etruscans held the field wherever there was educated taste. But no doubt Este was successful; she became the Italian Sheffield, and rivalled Bologna, which was now the Italian Birmingham, in supplying the foreign market. Each place produced perfectly good and perfectly uninteresting articles, of real commerical value but of no permanent importance.

It is not only in bronze work that the fourth century shows a decline from the fifth. Throughout the fifth century Este was producing a very handsome class of pottery quite unlike anything else in Italy. It is a ware painted with red ochre and graphite in alternate zones of cherry-red and lustrous black. This was justly admired and exported beyond the bounds of Venetia. But in the fourth century the manufacture was abandoned. Probably the demand for this ware was killed by the introduction of Attic painted vases. Bologna was full of the later red-figured Attic ware soon after 500 B.C., and some inferior examples have been found at Este towards the close of the fifth century, as well as some local copies which show that it came into fashion there.

As a factor of importance or interest in the history of art Este may be said to disappear from the scene soon after 400 B.C. But it maintained its political independence and continued to produce for the markets of Venetia and surrounding districts long after this.

The Atestine was the longest-lived of all the provincial Italian nationalities, and showed a singular tenacity even in its decadence. The student of history and manners may find much to interest him in the statuettes and plaques of the fourth and third centuries, though they have no artistic value. Este was vigorous and alive down to the days of the Roman Empire. The Romans never actually conquered it, but peacefully occupied Venetia in 184 B.C. Down to the beginning of the Christian era the Atestines retained their own language, dress, and customs.

CHAPTER 8

Golasecca and the Comacines

Paucity of material for archaeology of Lombardy. Early settlements round Lakes Maggiore and Como. Swords in tenth and ninth centuries were imported from north of the Alps. The cemeteries of Golasecca not Celtic. Are the Golaseccans and Comacines identical? Civilization of seventh and sixth centuries dependent principally on commerce with Trieste. In the fifth century Lombardy was the forwarding centre for Etruscan and Greek products. The Ligurian colonists as transport agents.

IN comparison with the archaeology of Venetia, which was described in the last chapter, that of Lombardy appears somewhat vague and ill defined. This is perhaps principally due to the very different character of the evidence. At Este careful and methodical excavations were made for many years. In Lombardy, however, the cemeteries around the Lago Maggiore and Lago di Como, which are the principal centres of interest, were unsystematically ransacked for nearly a century, and only a very few careful scientific studies were made. To weld so many fragmentary observations into a whole is not easy, in spite of all that the admirable Archaeological Society of Como has done in the way of salvage. The two small collections formed in the museums of Milan and Como, eked out by some valuable specimens at

Turin, and the scanty products of some recent excavations near Novara, constitute the principal basis for any deductions that I shall attempt.

Round the great lakes of Maggiore and Como settlements were made during the Iron Age by branches of that same mid-European and Danubian stock which in Romagna, Etruria, and Latium developed into the two Villanovan nations, while in Venetia it produced the Atestines. There is just enough evidence from Varese and Como to show that the migration into these parts began at the very dawn of the Iron Age, and to justify the assertion that there was an early period there corresponding to the First and Second Benacci. The burial rite was of course cremation, and the usual form of tomb at this time was a square shelter of stone slabs sunk from eighteen inches to five feet below the surface of the ground. In this was placed the pottery ossuary containing the cremated ashes and a few objects.

The only important or remarkable aspect of this period, so far as can be judged from the scanty material available, is the unexpected and perfectly diagnostic character of the weapons. Half a dozen superb bronze swords were found, every one of which was obviously a foreign importation. One type is the antennae sword, which has been mentioned in previous chapters, the other is a definitely Hungarian form. These are sufficient to show that a very close connexion was maintained, in the tenth and ninth centuries, between the Comacines and those transalpine countries from which they derived their origin. And, as it is only natural to infer that the line of commerce followed the path of the original migration, it is reasonable to conclude that the Comacines did not trickle down in small numbers through any and every pass of the Alps, but that they followed a perfectly definite line from east to west. The distribution of the swords is significant; it points all the way up from the southern end of Lake Como to Sondrio, and suggests that the route which was followed after leaving the Brenner came down to the lake by the Val di Sole and the Valtellina.

The next question that arises is whether the Golaseccans of Lago Maggiore came into the country from the same quarter. Their cemeteries are situated at the southern end of Lago Maggiore, where the river Ticino issues from the lake. Here is the Somma plateau, where the site of Golasecca is really only a part of the huge necropolis that is generally called by its name. At one time the theory was put forward that these settlements on the Somma plateau represented an exceedingly early Gaulish invasion, carried out by hypothetical proto-Celts. In a well-known book which champions this view they are ascribed to the tenth century. But more recent study has shown this chronology to be impossible. The grave of Sesto Calende containing the situla on which the argument was principally based is not earlier than 500 B.C., and no part of the Golasecca cemeteries can be shown to be earlier than the seventh century. But the theory dies hard, so that Hoernes, who has been the best critic of the chronology, speaks of the Sesto Calende grave as belonging to a Gaulish warrior. It is a very difficult doctrine to accept, for the rite of burial is different; the Gauls of the east coast of Italy, where their graves are best known, were an inhuming, not a cremating people. And the weapons of the Sesto Calende tomb are quite unlike those usually associated with the Gauls.[1]

The peculiar feature of the Golasecca cemeteries is the use of stone circles to enclose the graves. Moreover, these stone circles are often approached by regular corridors of unhewn stones. It is a system which has a good deal of superficial resemblance to the megalithic remains in Brittany and other Celtic regions, even though the date is so much later. But it may be an error to lay too much stress on this feature, especially as stone circles are not unknown in Italy, where they were used by several sets of people who seem to be in no way ethnically related to one another. How-

[1] See *The Iron Age in Italy*, pp. 70–4, and Plate 14.

ever, it may be something more than a coincidence that the nearest equivalent to the Golasecca circles is found at Tolentino on the coast of the Adriatic. There is so much resemblance between the minor arts of Lombardy and Picenum that Tolentino might quite possibly be regarded as a small colony of Golaseccans which had established itself on the Adriatic.

The kernel of the question is really whether certain differences which can be observed between the Golaseccans and the Comacines in the sixth and seventh centuries amount to more than the natural divergences between distinct though related tribes. Seeing that the Comacine culture in its strictest sense is not confined to the Lake of Como, but extends past Varese to Valtravaglia on the actual shore of Lago Maggiore, I cannot reconcile myself to admitting a different origin for the inhabitants of each of the two great lakes. If, however, it is considered legitimate and necessary to separate the inhabitants of the Somma plateau from the other 'Comacines', then I should suggest that the best explanation of the megalithic style of the Golasecca tombs might be found in deriving it from Switzerland. On the Swiss plateaux, where incineration was the usual rite at this time, there are numerous tumuli which might be the prototypes of the circle graves at Golasecca.

All the cemeteries in Lombardy fall naturally into two periods, viz. before and after 500 B.C. For the same phenomenon occurs here that we have seen elsewhere; after 500 B.C. the Etruscan influence begins to permeate, and it became particularly strong in the north-western region, where there was no very vigorous native culture to rival it.

During the seventh and sixth centuries the civilization round the two great lakes is not very advanced and gives little evidence of any native originality. Fibulae, whether on Maggiore or Como, are all, with the exception of one local type, the same that were generally diffused at this time everywhere north of the Apennines. And all the ornaments and implements are of patterns well known elsewhere. In finer metal work the Comacines and Golaseccans were so far behindhand that their productions in 500 B.C. would have been thought extremely childish at Bologna or Este three hundred years earlier. The only original product of any interest is the local pottery of the Somma plateau, which was handsome enough to be occasionally exported. It is sometimes found at Este and is one of the very few pieces of evidence for traffic between Venetia and Lombardy, which seems to have been very slight. The really important commerce of the lakes was with quite another region, and is singularly interesting in the new ideas that it suggests as to ancient trade routes. For if we compare the general style of the small ornaments found at Golasecca, and at the southern end of Lake Como, with those of Picenum, as seen in the museums of Ancona and Ascoli, the resemblance is so extraordinary that it goes far beyond the possibilities of mere coincidence. The constant use of chainwork and of spiral finials is a marked feature of each locality, the actual detail in the pattern of some of the smaller pendants is identical, and some of the ornaments from Golasecca graves are virtually duplicates of those in the museum at Ascoli (Plate 11).

Having established this, we must next observe that objects of exactly the same class are found in Istria and in Bosnia. The inevitable conclusion is that the same manufacturers were supplying all these regions in spite of their distance from one another. Where, it may be asked, was the centre of production? It was no Etruscan place, for this style is quite unlike anything Etruscan. It was not Venetia, because very little of the kind has been found at Este. In view of the poverty of their inventive genius, it is hard to think that the Comacines can have produced these ornaments. The choice, therefore, must lie between Picenum and the Balkans. In any case, it is plain that during the sixth and probably the seventh century there was a very active trade of which the focus must have been near

Trieste. From this place there were sent out quantities of small torques, pendants, armlets, and ornaments all so similar that they must almost have been distributed by the same firms or agents. These were carried westward as far as Lago Maggiore, southward to Ancona, and eastward to Bosnia. It is a very interesting network of commerce which is thus revealed for the first time by comparing the products of these several regions.

In the fifth century native production in Lombardy had sunk to a very low point, and the whole province was almost entirely given up to the reception and forwarding of things made in other places. To the trade from Istria had now been added the trade from the Etruscan colonies. A regular system of transport had come into use by which Etruscan and Greek bronze vessels were sent along the line of Lago Maggiore to Bellinzona and thence over the Alpine passes to the upper waters of the Rhine. It was by this route that they found their way to Switzerland, Western Germany, France, Belgium, and even England. Near Bellinzona have been found the settlements of the transport agents, apparently a colony of Ligurians who migrated there from the Italian Riviera about the year 600 B.C. The contents of their graves are exactly what might be expected from their position. These Ligurians came to possess a good deal from Campania, a little

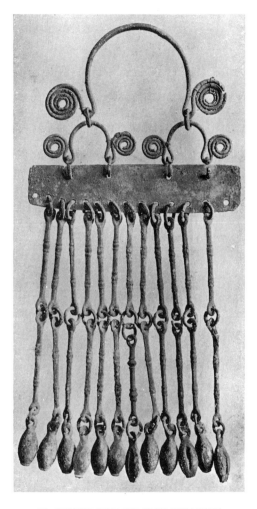

11. BRONZE PENDANT FROM GOLASECCA

from Etruria and Bologna, many small objects
from their neighbours on the Ticino and Lake
Como, and now and again a brooch or a pin
brought from the north side of the Alps. They
exhibited a certain dexterity in metal-working,
shown especially in the manufacture of bronze
belts, but their products were very primitive in
comparison with those of Central and Southern
Italy. These are the only Ligurians of whom
archaeology has anything to tell, and as they
formed a peculiar colony with special trade-con-
nexions they cannot be considered as genuinely
representative of Ligurian life. In regard to this
we must remain ignorant. Classical authors describe the Ligurians as a very primitive folk, and
probably they hardly enter as a factor of any importance into the pre-history of Italy. Nor can it
be said that the Golaseccans and Comacines really
added anything to the 'patrimonio artistico' of the
country as a whole, though the study of their
character and fortunes from their first migration
to the Gaulish invasion is interesting as a phase
of early history.

CHAPTER 9

The Picenes of the East Coast

Use of the name Picene and its connotation. The Picenes were descendants of the Neolithic people. Their burial custom was not cremation but inhumation. The east coast owed its development at first to Istria and the Balkans, afterwards to Greece. The Picenes were primarily warriors—their weapons and the sources whence these were derived. Decorated and inscribed stelae. Dress and ornaments. Trade with Magna Graecia and importation of Ionic bronzes and other Greek works.

THE Picenes are the people who lived in historic times on the coast of the Adriatic between Ancona and the mouth of the Sangro. On the west of them the classical atlas places the large province of Umbria, and to the south the whole country of the Samnites, extending almost from sea to sea and perpetually threatening Campania. Umbria and Picenum are included together under the single title of Picenes in the map given as Plate 3, because the culture of this entire region is homogeneous and must therefore be called by a single name. I have purposely avoided the use of the term 'Umbrian' because it has perfectly different meanings to different writers, and carries with it an atmosphere of prejudice inherited from controversies with which the reader need not be troubled. There is little objection to any one substituting the term 'Umbro-Picene', if he so desires, for my simpler 'Picene', but it hardly adds to clearness. South of the Sangro the Samnites are a factor of scarcely any importance in the history of civilization; they were a poor and hardy race of warriors, with no more interest in art or commerce than the earliest Romans in the fighting days of the Republic. In so far as they had any culture it was derived from the Picenes, through whom they obtained the few ornaments that their ascetic life allowed.

The Picenes, or Umbro-Picenes, were probably the oldest of the races whom we meet north of the latitude of Rome. There are some writers who consider that they only settled in their Italian homes at some time in the Bronze Age; but it is more natural and consistent with the evidence to regard them as descendants of the Neolithic inhabitants, who had never shifted from their original lands. They retained the custom of burying their dead in the ground, which marks the first great point of contrast between them and the cremating Villanovans or Atestines. But the difference between the transalpine invaders and the aboriginal survivors on the east of the Apennines is not confined to burial customs; the whole orientation of their life is different. The Picene looked as naturally up and down the Adriatic as the Etrurian looked over the Tyrrhene sea. The development of the west coast comes from its commerce with the Aegean through the Straits of Messina; but the earliest history of the east coast is bound up in its connexion with Istria and the Balkans, while its later and richer civilization is due to land trade with Magna Graecia.

Thus in the first graves of the eleventh or twelfth century B.C., whether found near Pesaro or in Ancona itself, there appear types which are unknown west of the Apennines or north of Rimini. The 'spectacle fibula', made of a pair of spiral volutes, is a form well known in Greece and the Balkans, but virtually absent from the west coast. At Terni, where the Picenes from the beginning of the Iron Age maintained a border post to protect the passes, some of the early fibulae are actually Hungarian.

The available material for study is scanty before the eighth century, after which, however, there is sufficient for a very complete review. In the eighth and seventh centuries, as revealed by the cemeteries of Novilara near Pesaro, the most salient characteristic that appears is the extraordinarily warlike character of the Picenes. That the Samnites were fierce warriors is well known from history, but the pugnacious disposition of the Picenes would not have been suspected if it had not been for the contents of their graves. In these cemeteries practically every man's grave contained weapons, and they often made up quite a formidable armoury. The favourite arm was the spear; in the Servici cemetery only four out of thirty-seven graves had not at least one spear, while twelve had more than one. Only half as frequent as the spear was the dagger, of which there were several varieties. Swords, which were peculiarly characteristic in form, were somewhat rarer, being only found in ten graves. Helmets were rather less common than swords, and only one shield has been detected.

If this armoury is examined it proves to be extraordinarily interesting for the connexion that it reveals. A Picene warrior, when he went out to battle, perhaps to repel a foray of the Villanovans or Etruscans, looked something like a foot-soldier as painted on a Dipylon vase, who had apparently swapped half his weapons in Bosnia for the local Balkan models. The most curious thing was his sword, if he had one. This was purely Bosnian, quite unlike any form known elsewhere in Greece or in Italy. I show a picture of it in Plate 12, no. 3. It is a heavy chopping weapon, made of iron, with a broad back and the cutting edge on the under side; the handle is set on to the blade at an obtuse angle. The sheath was of wood, covered with sheets of bronze handsomely engraved or decorated in openwork, and must have looked very well as it hung from the belt.

Other forms of swords, however, were also used, some of purely Greek models as they are known to us from the vase paintings. Evidently the Picene generals did not insist on standardization, but allowed a certain latitude in the choice of arms. They were justified by the results, for the Picenes successfully maintained their independence until the third century B.C. It was only after the war with Pyrrhus that Rome felt strong enough to humble them.

Daggers in the eighth and seventh centuries were of no less than three varieties. One, which is a common Hallstatt form, needs no description; but the type shown in Plate 12, no. 2, is quite individual and peculiar. Its iron hilt and iron sheath were decorated with bosses of bronze, and the sheath terminated in a series of bulbs, all of iron except the lowest, which was bronze. Helmets at this date were of a conical form, with a crest and plume much resembling those shown in Dipylon vase-paintings. Other types of helmets were added in the sixth and fifth centuries, during which time the choice and variety of weapons was greatly increased, so that the tombs round Ancona contained many new forms. In these there were nine different kinds of spears and several new types of swords and daggers, beside javelins and maces. At the same time the defensive armour was increased by the use of greaves and breast-

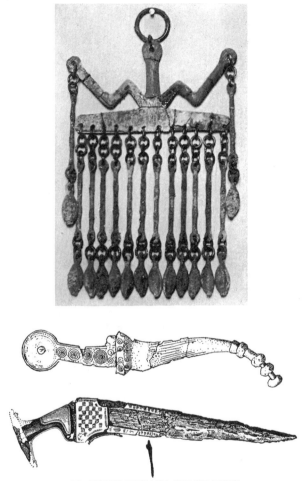

12. PICENE PENDANT AND WEAPONS

plates. Chariots of Greek pattern were also introduced for the use of the leaders.

It was not only on land that the Picenes had to
fight. Some curious stelae of the seventh century
show not only warriors and hunters with their
weapons, but also something which is much more
important, namely the ships of the period. A
rudely incised drawing on one stone depicts a large
galley fitted with mast and square sail as well as
with oars, while below it two smaller row-boats
are involved in a contest prow to prow. This may
well be the record of one of those engagements
with Liburnian pirates which were probably frequent enough in the Adriatic. On some of these
tombstones, which are ornamented with spiral
designs in thoroughly Picene style, are inscriptions
written in the Sabellian language, which may
possibly give the epitaphs of the more famous
men. The alphabet in which they are expressed
is related to the early Greek and Etruscan.

For dress in Picenum there is some direct as
well as indirect evidence in the tombs of the sixth
and fifth centuries, in which the fabric of the gar-
ments was sometimes preserved. The men wore a
single coarse robe of wool fastened with countless
fibulae. But the women were dressed in a large
mantle covering a sleeved tunic, and the upper
part of this mantle was dotted all over with tiny
gewgaws such as rings of bronze, glass beads,

amber and ivory trinkets. Their girdles consisted
of a narrow strip of what looks like chain-mail, but
is really only an arrangement of bronze rings, not
interlinked but merely sewn together.   Chainwork was the principal element in their pendants
and pectorals, made of several rows of bronze
rings hanging from a spacer shaped like a double-
headed bird, or more rarely like a pair of human
arms (Plate 12). Torques and armlets, both of
which are very frequent, were apparently worn by
men as well as women, and it may be particularly
noted that they were not introduced by the Gauls,
who had not yet descended upon Italy. Beginning
as a plain wire circlet, the torque in the fifth century becomes an exquisite ornament with beautiful
finials shaped as animals' heads or the figures of
horses.

Many of the smaller ornaments, as well as the
more elaborate pectorals and chatelaines, are absolutely identical with those used by the Comacines.
I have already suggested that the probable explanation is to be found in a system of commerce
which, during the sixth century and probably
earlier, must have passed up the Adriatic to the
head of the Gulf of Venice, where it branched off
by land routes to the east and to the west. On
the whole, I am disposed to think that the centre
of manufacture was rather in Picenum than in the
Balkans, though each region may have contri-

buted its quota. Actual moulds for casting some
of the pendants have been found in the Picene
cemeteries; and it is evident that considerable
production of some kind was absolutely necessary,
to enable the Picenes to pay for the amber, which
they used on a scale unparalleled elsewhere in
Italy.

A revolution in the appreciation of art was
brought about by the trade with Magna Graecia,
which began in the sixth century and reached its
zenith in the fifth. The cemeteries round Ancona
have produced some of the finest specimens of
early Greek art known in Italy. Bronze bowls and
censers, bas-reliefs on greaves and shields, carvings
in ivory and amber, represent the finest craftsman-
ship of the contemporary Greek world. In Plate 13
is illustrated a bronze disk which represents two
mounted horsemen armed with spears and wearing helmets, one of whom is thrusting his spear
into a prostrate enemy who carries a round shield
and a mace. Another disk in the same style shows
two foot-soldiers armed with daggers and locked
in a mortal struggle. The handles of bronze vessels
are ornamented with groups of figures, showing
Herakles as the horse-tamer and a pair of lions
on his shoulders, or heroes fighting like Hector
and Achilles over the body of Patroclus. Nothing
is more instructive than to contrast these imported
works with the native situlae produced at the

same time, infantile works which would be thought crude in the wilds of Africa. To judge by these the Picenes were entirely deficient in precisely that craft in which the Villanovans so particularly excelled. All their larger bronzes were always imported. In the seventh century the types show that they obtained ribbed cists, censers, and bronze tables from Etruria; a century later they were mainly dependent on South Italy.

A little before 500 B.C., then, the Picene, while remaining a fierce warrior, had been carried away by the fascination of Greek art and filled his country with the finest products that Tarentum could send. The objects of minor art are no less beautiful than the bronzes. There are carvings of animals in ivory or amber, ivory statuettes and innumerable other exquisite objects from Belmonte and other cemeteries. These are still unpublished but may be seen in the museum at Ancona.

It was by way of Apulia, and not by direct trade with Greece, that Greek art penetrated into Picenum. This is proved by the occurrence of Apulian painted pottery, which is quite unmistakable and will be described in the next chapter. Greek painted vases are less numerous than might have been expected, though there are a certain number of specimens, ranging in date from the proto-Corinthian of the seventh century down to the late red-figured style of 450 B.C.

13. BRONZE DISK WITH IONIC BAS-RELIEF

The curious native pottery suggests an idea which may be worth recording. In a great number of instances the pots are surmounted by the figures of an ox or have handles in the form of a pair of oxen conjoined. Even when the original shape has been lost the horns are still retained. Similarly, among the women's ornaments, small models of oxen are quite common. I cannot but suspect that there was some religious idea in this, perhaps an old Italian cult of some god of cattle.

It would be interesting but too long to follow Greek art of the fourth century as it is seen in Picenum. The finest examples of that period are to be found not among the Sabellian population but in the tombs of their neighbours the Senonian Gauls. These parvenus, fresh from the capture of Rome, settled between Rimini and Ancona in the first half of the fourth century B.C. With their huge plunder they were rich enough to hire the best craftsmen of the day. The gold of which their torques and crowns and armlets were made was perhaps the very gold which the Senate and people of Rome had paid as a ransom to Brennus. It was fashioned by the Greek artist into objects so beautiful that we can hardly rank as barbarians the warrior chiefs who wore them.

CHAPTER 10

Apulia. Greeks, Daunians, and others

Greek tombs of the seventh century containing figured
bronzes. In these tombs was also indigenous pottery. Such
pottery is the only source for our knowledge of native
Apulian life. Distinction between schools of pottery. The
Daunian painted vases and fantastic vases. The Peucetian.
The later school of Canosa. Importance of Canosa in the
Hellenistic period.

SINCE we have seen that Picenum was filled
with Greek art in the fifth and sixth centuries,
we might have expected to find that Apulia,
which was nearer to Tarentum, was still richer.
And no doubt in course of time the buried treasures
of this province will come to light. But at present
exploration in the south-east of Italy is still in its
infancy; so that the newly founded museum of
Bari, though interesting in many ways, has far
less to teach than that of Ancona. Even Taranto
itself, which has beautiful and valuable series of
pottery and small objects from the Corinthian
period downward, possesses few early works of
major importance.

Under these circumstances the discovery of four
intact Greek tombs dating from the end of the
seventh century at Noicattaro, a little south-east
of Bari, was an event of great interest. Three of
them contained only Corinthian pottery, mixed
with examples of the indigenous painted wares
which will presently be described, but the fourth

had figured bronzes which are unique examples
of the Corinthian work of the period. The grave
was a monolithic sarcophagus, only about four
and a half feet long, from which it follows that the
body must have been buried in a contracted position. Outside the sarcophagus were eight pieces of
the indigenous painted ware and four Corinthian
vases. One of them was decorated with such well-
known motives as palmettos and lotus flowers,
another with a single zone of animals showing
a swan or winged harpy and a pair of wild boars
charging one another. These are sufficient to
establish the date with approximate accuracy.
The pottery was covered with a round shield of
bronze, ornamented in repoussé with a pattern
like basket-work and a row of scaraboids. Inside
the sarcophagus were the two figured bronzes, a
long narrow plaque, and a girdle, together with a
bronze jug, a pair of greaves, and the fragments of
an iron spear and iron sword.

The plaque was about five inches wide and had
been cut into two pieces before being deposited
in the grave. It was divided into eight panels, of
which the first represents a pair of sphinxes and
the last a pair of lions, while the other six repeat
twice over the same three mythological scenes.
These are the fight between Achilles and Pen-
thesilea, Herakles slaying the Nemean lion, and
Theseus slaying the Minotaur. Ionic volutes and

a very beautiful palmetto terminate each end. This plaque, which may have been the covering either of a girdle or of a sword-sheath, belongs to a small and very important class of Greek bronzes other examples of which have been found at Dodona, Orchomenos, Olympia, the Acropolis, Delphi, and Aegina. An extensive critical literature has been devoted to them, and it has been much debated to what particular school they should be assigned. Gervasio, who has written the authoritative memoir on the Noicattaro tomb, adduces good reasons for classing this example at least as Corinthian. Even finer, from the artistic standpoint, than the plaque is a figured girdle, nearly three and a half feet long and five inches wide. On it are depicted in repoussé work six quadrigae or four-horse chariots racing with one another.

For the chronology and study of the indigenous pottery it has been very useful to find some of the most representative specimens in Greek graves like that of Noicattaro. Unfortunately, however, there are only very few instances in which these graves were excavated by scientific workers.

For a long while collections of native Apulian pottery existing in different museums in Europe have been very much misunderstood and misdated. The study, however, has recently been put on a thoroughly sound basis, so that it is possible to separate the several schools and to assign a very close dating to each. This is all the more necessary as the only information of any kind that we can obtain for native Apulia in the Iron Age is derived from the pottery. Even the interesting local civilization of Molfetta cannot be traced after the beginning of the Bronze Age. Except for the peculiar and isolated site of Timmari, which is in no sense characteristic, there is a sheer gap of something like a thousand years, until the pottery of the seventh century appears. It is impossible to prophesy what future excavation may bring to light, but it seems almost certain that the Early Iron Age in Apulia will eventually prove to be quite unlike anything that has been described in the preceding chapters. Meanwhile we must be content to derive what suggestions we can as to the character and abilities of the several Apulian tribes from the study of their pottery, which is more interesting than any of the other Italian ware of the same period.

Setting aside the isolated finds of early geometric pottery made at Taranto and near Manfredonia, which are unrelated to anything else and cannot yet be explained, it may be said that the earliest Apulian wares begin about 650 B.C. We are able to date them principally from their relation to early Greek tombs such as that of Noicattaro, but a check on the dating is provided in some instances by the finding of exported specimens in Picene graves.

Three schools must be clearly distinguished as Northern, Central, and Southern. It is usual to give them the names of the tribes which occupied these different regions, who were known to the Romans as Daunians, Peucetians, and Messapians. The Daunian wares run from 600 to 450, and were produced principally at Canosa and Ruvo. A large collection of them may be seen in the museum of Bari, but there is also an important series at Taranto, and there are specimens in various collections outside Italy. The most curious type is a two-storied jar with side-handles, to which a third and a fourth handle are added of increasingly fantastic character as time goes on. These handles are made to resemble an animal's face, something like an owl or a cat, or sometimes a human hand. The hand was probably a talisman; it is often employed in North African ornaments even at the present day.[1]

Hardly less strange is no. 2 in Plate 14, which was probably a ritual vase of some kind and really looks more Peruvian than Italian. It is decorated with the usual geometrical patterns, and also with the rare motive of wild sheep on the hills. But the

[1] For illustrations of this and other Apulian pottery the reader should look up Plates 42–7 of *The Iron Age in Italy.*

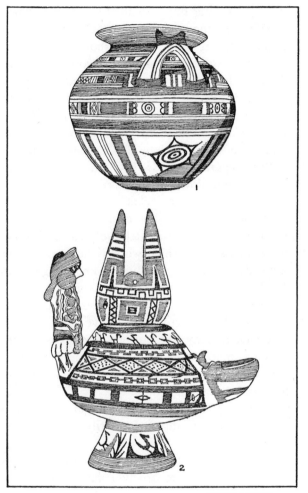

14. APULIAN PAINTED POTTERY. DAUNIAN SCHOOL

most interesting thing about it is a female figure moulded in the round and attached to the side opposite to the spout. She is shown in the ceremonial dress of a priestess or woman of rank. Around the brow is a high fillet, and long plaits of hair hang down on the shoulders, while the ears are covered each with a circular disk. A long pendent ornament of disks hangs down in front, and there are indications of a necklace composed of three separate strands. Over the eyes is a black mask coming down to the nose. The dress consists of two parts, a jacket and a pleated skirt. Such documents for the dress and manners of the period are unfortunately very rare; they are the material from which we may hope to recover some day a certain amount of knowledge as to Apulian life. Other ritual vases are even more fantastic, with birds' heads on a sort of neck like some antediluvian creature. I have illustrated this specimen to show the curious fanciful character which comes out in so much of the indigenous Daunian. But a more characteristic example of the usual style is no. 1 in Plate 14, which has a quiet scheme of geometrical design arranged with a good eye for spacing and distribution over the field.

The Peucetian pottery is very different from the Daunian. There are two main classes: the first consisting of wares painted in black on a

white slip, with a very sober and restricted scheme
of decoration which is purely native and unaffected by Greek motives. This probably begins
as early as 650 B.C. A little later is a very handsome red and black ware which is found in the
same tombs with actual Corinthian craters. It is
exceedingly interesting to see the reaction of the
Peucetian mind as exhibited in a specimen like
Plate 15, no. 1. The native potter has taken the
idea of a frieze of griffins or birds like turkeys,
which is so characteristic of early Corinthian pottery, and has combined it with his own designs.
These designs had become traditional long before
the arrival of the Greeks; the most characteristic
of them is the comb, and almost equally common is the swastika. Lozenges, chess-boards, and
square maeanders, all of which appear in different
combinations, are a survival from the earliest days
of geometric art in Europe. The Peucetians inherited, in short, from very early times a few simple
motives, and worked them into a whole which is
the expression of their own temperament and their
own racial psychology. It is a simple, ascetic, and
very dignified art which emerges from this expression. The genius of the Daunians is totally different. It is varied, quick, adaptable, fanciful,
delighting in fresh ideas and not shrinking from the
grotesque. Both schools exhibit the highest artistic
capacity and react with complete freedom against

the influence of the foreigner, which never en-
slaved them.

As contrasted with these, the Messapian school,
though pretty enough in some ways, is not interesting because it is entirely permeated with Greek
feeling. I shall disregard it here for that reason,
and speak rather of another school, which combined with late Hellenism a conspicuous degree
of independence.

An interval of more than a century separates
even the earliest of the Late Canosan pottery from
the true Daunian and the Peucetian, both of which
had died out before 450 B.C. Canosa, which had
been one of the principal centres of the earlier
Daunian manufacture, underwent a total revolution of artistic feeling between 500 and 300 B.C.
A vase like that which is shown in Plate 15, no. 2,
must be dated to the third century, and shows a
union of completely Greek decoration with a form
that is purely native. This hybridization is quite
typical of the whole school, the extreme chrono-
logical limits of which lie between 350 and 200
B.C. In this period of a hundred or a hundred
and fifty years the little Apulian town asserted
its vitality and independence in a renascence
of extraordinary vigour. It became one of the
centres of the Hellenistic world, and if we cannot
always admire its taste we must admit the extraordinary brilliancy and fecundity of its invention.

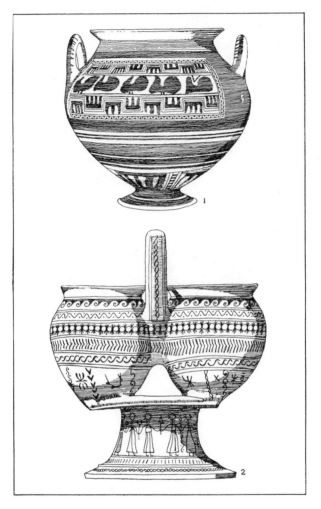

15. APULIAN POTTERY. I. PEUCETIAN ; 2. LATE CANOSAN

With a great deal of minor pottery, very fairly
represented by the double-situla of Plate 15,
Canosa was now producing huge polychrome
terra-cottas which were widely admired in the contemporary world. In many European museums,
and especially at Naples, may be seen these aston-
ishing rococo compositions, large vases with centaurs
and cupids springing from the sides and sometimes
a Niobe or a Hermes surmounting them. Separate
figures such as a mourning woman are sometimes
exhibited as statuettes detached from the original
groups, and in such cases we are sometimes sur-
prised into irresistible admiration of their beauty.

Canosa had now become so wealthy that it was
like a second Tarentum for luxury and magnificence. The masses of coloured glass, gold work,
jewellery, pottery, and bronze now buried in any
grave demanded much space to house them.
Accordingly the simpler tomb of earlier times became a wide chamber, entered by a passage that
led down to a door sculptured with fine architectural details. In such family vaults as these were
laid the wealthy Daunians who lived in the time of
the Egyptian Ptolemies. Around them stood price-
less Greek vases painted with the story of Darius,
or with scenes from epic or mythology, beside
which the merchant princes of Canosa did not
disdain to place the handiwork of their own fellow
citizens.

CHAPTER II

Cumae and Campania

Campanian history centres around Cumae. Date of the founding of Cumae. Chief material for judging native civilization comes from a few pre-Hellenic graves. These are principally of the eighth century. The most important inference to be drawn is that there are no Villanovans. The pre-Hellenic Campanians were quite unconnected with the invaders of North and Central Italy. Relations between Greeks and Etruscans in Campania. Foundation of Capua and resultant wars ending in defeat of Etruscans. Importance of Greek colony of Cumae was very great, but it must not be considered the sole gate for Greek commerce with Italy. The twin schools of painted pottery at Cumae and Corneto.

THE beginnings of Campanian history centre about the very important Greek colony of Cumae, and almost everything that can be learned of the prehistoric period is based on the excavations made at this single place. Historians have been somewhat nebulous as to the date of the foundation of Cumae. Strabo states that it was the oldest of all the Greek colonies whether in Sicily or on the mainland, but this need not necessarily place the beginnings of the settlement before the second half of the eighth century. For in Sicily, where the dates are pretty well established by literary evidence, it is known that the first colony was Syracuse, which was founded in 734

B.C. The Greek writer Eusebius, however, says that Cumae was colonized in 1050 B.C., and though most historians have hesitated to accept such a remarkable statement, more than one leading archaeologist has welcomed it. It has sometimes been supposed that the excavations at Cumae could be shown to support Eusebius; but, on the contrary, an analysis of the contents of the earliest Greek graves shows that not one of them is earlier than 700 B.C. The fantastic dating to the eleventh century therefore falls to the ground, and we can return to the sober opinion that Cumae was actually founded about the year 740 B.C. If Greek prospectors made occasional landings on this part of the coast some generations before this, which is not at all impossible, the places where they settled have not yet been found. Strabo and Livy suggest that Ischia and Procida were tentatively selected by the first comers, but this may have been only a year or two before the Chalcidians wisely decided on the admirable site about twelve miles west of Naples, which became the most important Greek city in Italy. Doubtless they chose it not only for its nearness to the sea but for its capabilities of defence. Whether in Sicily or in Italy, the first Greek colonists were always settling on the outskirts of a native population which might be far from friendly. They took the same sort of chance as the first English colonists in America, who might happen to come upon friendly Indians but might very likely fall in with an implacable and relentless enemy. It is quite clear that the Cumaeans were not a warlike people, and that they took no steps to conquer the natives of Campania even in the immediate neighbourhood. The seventh-century graves of the indigenous inhabitants, in the valley of the Sarno near Pompeii, show that these tribes maintained their own manner of life quite undisturbed and not much affected by the arrival of the foreigners.

There is very little evidence, however, for the life and character of the native Campanians before the eighth century. Practically the only material for the pre-Hellenic time is derived from forty-two graves which came to light in the process of exploring the Greek cemetery itself. To this can be added only some fragments of information obtained from bungled unscientific digging at Suessula, and a few fibulae and small objects from the neighbourhood of the place that was afterwards Capua. Nearly all the pre-Hellenic graves belong to the eighth century and only a very few to the ninth or earlier. They contained a great quantity of the hand-made black pottery, which occurs all over Italy and is probably an inheritance from the Bronze Age. In Campania there is a good deal of resemblance to the forms found in the pottery of Latium in the same period, but

there are also some original varieties that do not
occur as far north as the Tiber.

A little more information can be obtained from
the fibulae, as at Cumae, Capua, and Suessula
there are several types never found north of Campania ; while the whole series shows more affinity
with the east and south coasts than with the
Latian styles. Some Egyptian scarabs, faience,
and figurines demonstrate the existence of trade
with the Aegean. Finally there are pendants
obtained from sporadic diggings, of which there
is no official record, so closely resembling the
Picene types described in my last chapter that
they must have been obtained from the same source.

Scanty as this information is, a few points emerge
quite clearly, the most important of which is that
there is no trace of Villanovan settlement, and
hardly any trace of Villanovan influence. The
positive boundary between the northern and
southern peoples of Italy in the Early Iron Age
must be placed very near Monte Circeo. Villanovan graves have been found at Anzio, but south
of this they are unknown, so that the Campanians
were evidently quite unrelated to the cremating
invaders of North and Central Italy. Whether they
were of the same stock as the Neolithic people who
preceded the invaders cannot yet be determined.
Their material civilization, however, which was
probably not very original or important as a native

product, was distinctly affected by currents coming both from the Aegean and from the Adriatic.

When the Chalcidians from Euboea first landed at Cumae they fround the Etruscans already in possession of the coast between the Arno and the Tiber and a certain amount of the interior behind it. South of this they had not advanced before the end of the eighth century; but they were powerful and dangerous neighbours, even though separated from Cumae by a long strip of neutral territory. For more than a century there are no signs of enmity between Greeks and Etruscans, and there is some indication that the two peoples maintained peaceful commercial relations. Occasional pieces of Etruscan gold jewellery have been found in Greek tombs of the seventh century, and there is the very remarkable instance of the grave of a wealthy Etruscan being found on the site of Cumae itself. It is dated by its contents, which exactly duplicate some of the objects found in the Regolini-Galassi and contemporary Etruscan tombs, to the middle of the seventh century. As there is not the slightest reason to suppose that the Etruscans were in possession of Cumae at this time, we can only conclude that some trader or agent had settled there for political or commercial purposes. The extraordinary case of the Etruscan mummy found at Alexandria in Egypt, though later in date, supplies a possible analogy.

At the end of the seventh century, however, the Etruscans, now masters of Rome, began to adopt a policy of aggression. It was about 600 B.C. that they founded Capua and began to menace the Greek colony. From this moment the enmity between Greeks and Etruscans was open and declared. In 524 Capua, with the aid of the Daunians and Aurunci, attacked Cumae. The Cumaeans defeated them and promptly allied themselves with the Latins, whom they assisted to defeat their Etruscan rivals at Ariccia. Soon after this, Rome, freed from the Tarquins, re-established the Latin League, and thereby drove a wedge between Etruria and Campania. The Syracusans, coming to the aid of their Greek kinsmen, defeated the Etruscan navy in sight of Cumae itself in 474 B.C., and the Chalcidian colony was then finally freed from the menace of its northern neighbours. But less than fifty years later the irresistible Samnites from the mountains overwhelmed both Capua and Cumae, and founded a composite state in which the language became Oscan though the dominant civilization naturally remained Greek as heretofore.

From 700 to 400 B.C., therefore, the study of Campania is practically the study of Cumae, for the Etruscan domination left few permanent traces. The importance of this Greek colony in the development of Italian culture west of the Apennines was very great; but it is possible to exaggerate it, and I think there is a general tendency to exaggerate it. Cumae was not the only place through which Oriental or Greek objects could find their way into Western Italy. The Etruscan ports had been carrying on an extensive commerce with the Aegean for fully a century before Cumae was founded; and the establishment of this small Chalcidian colony was not such an epoch-making event that it was likely to deflect trade from its well-established routes, especially as Cumae was far weaker in military force than any of the Etruscan states. There are not infrequent traces of Greek, as distinguished from Oriental, imports in Etruria itself during the eighth if not the ninth century. It is natural, in fact, to suppose that well before 800 B.C. ports of call were established which soon became a regular series echelonned all the way up the western coast. Oriental and Greek traders would make it their habit to call at each of these in order. It was more or less like the establishment of the Portuguese factories round the coast of Africa in the sixteenth century. At each port the trading ship would unload some part of its merchandise and receive whatever was due in exchange. Etruria could give iron and copper, the materials most sought and desired; what Cumae could give is not clear, unless it was some product peculiar to the volcanic region in which it was situated.

This question of trade-routes is brought into prominence by the interesting fact that at Caere, Vulci, and Corneto there have been found numerous painted vases of indubitably Greek origin, which are so similar to those of Cumae that some of them at least must have issued from the same factory. The date of this class of ware is well established as extending from 700 to 650 B.C., soon after which it was generally replaced by the Corinthian, at least in Etruria. In Plate 16 are reproduced two jars from Corneto and two from Cumae to show that if the industries are not identical they are at least twin sisters. But in spite of the close general similarity of the two classes there are some individual types found in Etruria which do not occur at Cumae. This suggests a variation in local taste, if not actually a choice of different makers, and makes it doubtful whether the commerce with Etruria always or necessarily passed through Cumae. I have already suggested that there was no particular reason why it should; for the same ship which brought a cargo to the Bay of Naples could perfectly well continue its voyage to the port of Corneto. So long as Chalcidians and Etruscans were still on friendly terms there could be no object in transhipping, and we know that this pottery was never transported by land, as it is entirely absent from the region between Capua and the Tiber.

Once the original models had found their way
into Italy, however, they could readily be copied;
and it is an interesting question, by no means
easy to answer, whether any factories for producing imitations were ever opened in Etruria. There
are three possibilities: either the Etruscan cities
may have continued to import direct from Greece,
or they may have manufactured for themselves, or
they may have obtained a supply direct from the
potters at Cumae, who probably did set up on
their own account before long.

It is an unsolved question in what part of Greece
the original manufactory of this ware was situated.
Gabrici, who has written the official monograph
on the excavations, assumes that it was in Euboea, at Chalcis, the mother-city of Cumae. The
assumption is very natural, but lacks proof because
the original Euboean pottery is still unknown.
So that it may be somewhat premature to label
as ' Chalcidian ' these very beautiful wares, of
which my two examples give only a slight idea.
This Cumaean pottery of the seventh century is
exceedingly attractive. It is made on the wheel,
and is composed of a finely purified clay of reddish
colour, coated with a pale slip on which simple
designs are painted in black. If these designs are
analysed it will be found that there is an un-
dercurrent of rectilinear geometrical decoration
inherited from the earliest Iron Age. But this tra-

16. PAINTED VASE. 1, 2 from CORNETO; 3, 4 from CUMAE

dition becomes more and more subordinated to the use of new schemes, floral and zoomorphic. With plant forms and the palmetto there are soon associated fishes, stags, horses, and serpents. It is a vivid and rich repertoire, indicative of a highly artistic people intensely interested in decoration and design. The spirit is so like that expressed in the early Corinthian pottery that after the first generation the work of a Cumaean draughtsman might almost be mistaken for Corinthian. But the peculiar hall-marks of the Corinthian school are absent, so that the 'Chalcidian' must be recognized as a distinct and peculiar product.

In the sixth century Attic influence begins to assert itself at Cumae as well as elsewhere, so that the peculiar characterization of this city is somewhat obscured. The culture of its classical period may be fully studied in the museum of Naples.

CHAPTER 12

Calabria and the Calabro-Siculans

Geographic connotation of the name Calabria. Importance of new discoveries in extreme south. Relative positions of Torre Galli and Canale. Difference in degree of Greek influence due to topographical conditions. What was the original native background in the Bronze Age? At least it was not Villanovan in any strict sense. Traffic between Torre Galli and Campania. Difference of customs between Calabrians and Villanovans. The Calabrians were of Siculan origin. Proof of this in the character of the rock-tombs. But no intercourse between even the most southern part of Italy and Sicily. Geometric Greek vases at Canale. Native weapons at Torre Galli. Differences between the two sites in regard to ornaments as well as weapons.

THE name Calabria might easily be misleading to any one who is accustomed to think primarily in terms of ancient history. It is necessary to remember that the name applied in Roman days to the country of the Messapians was transferred, in the eighth century after Christ, from the heel of Italy to the front part of the foot. In medieval and modern geography Calabria means a province extending from the south of the Gulf of Policastro to the Straits of Messina, corresponding therefore to the ancient Bruttium together with most of Lucania. It is in this sense that the term will be used in the present chapter.

The discoveries made by Orsi during the last few years have thrown the most unexpected light on a part of this province, and bid fair to give a wholly new orientation to all our ideas as to the pre-Hellenic history of Southern Italy. Torre Galli and Canale, the two principal sites which he has excavated in the mountains between Catanzaro and Reggio, will henceforth be the standard of reference for the whole archaeology of the south. In short, they will probably become for all Italy south of Rome what Bologna has long been for the north and centre.

Torre Galli is situated on the plateau of Monte Leone, overlooking the Tyrrhene Sea. Canale and the minor sites adjoining it form a group on the outskirts of the Greek colony of Locri, near the place marked on the map as Gerace. The difference of geographical position had the most important effect on the respective history and development of the two places. They are separated by a tract of precipitous mountain, covered in ancient times with deep forest which made communications extremely difficult. All the natural trade-routes and connexions of Torre Galli lie on the west side of the mountains, linking it with Campania and the western side of Central Italy. But Canale turns its back to the Italian peninsula and looks down immediately upon the Ionian Sea, whose waters were ploughed, even before the days

of Homer, by adventurers and explorers sailing
from Greece or the Levant. Behind the riviera
that became Magna Graecia rose the irregular
hinterland of cliffs and broken plateaux. It was
here that the natives dwelt.

It follows naturally from the difference of position that the inhabitants of the native villages
about Canale were affected much earlier and
more strongly by Greek influences than their
kinsmen at Torre Galli, who were isolated by
their remoteness. Doubtless a certain amount of
commerce passed to and fro over the mountain
roads, difficult though they were, that connected
the Ionian with the Tyrrhene Sea. But this had
little effect upon the inhabitants of the Tyrrhene
side, who remained essentially Italian, while those
on the east of the mountains were first allured by
the bait of Greek merchandise, and then, after
some generations, succumbed to the force of Greek
arms. Canale and the other indigenous villages
on the outskirts of Locri were obliterated by the
jealous Locrians in the early part of the seventh
century, but Torre Galli survived till about 500
B.C. At this date Locri finally achieved the aim
of her policy, which was to master and monopo-
lize the trade-route between the two seas. Upon
the control of this shortened land-passage into
Western Italy, by which merchandise from Greece
could pass without risking the dangers of the

Straits of Messina, depended much of the commercial prosperity of the Greek colony.

Locri Epizephyrii was founded about 680 B.C., but the native communities with which this chapter is concerned had existed for at least two centuries before that time. We are able to trace the life of the pre-Hellenic people for about four hundred years at Torre Galli, and two hundred years at Canale. Fundamentally the civilization in the two districts is identical; it must belong to the same race and to tribes that were very near akin; but on the background of common inheritance the compelling forces of geography wove two very different patterns.

First, then, I will discuss the question of this background of common inheritance. Whence was it derived, and with what else is it connected? Orsi has picturesquely phrased a traditional view which ought only to be accepted with distinct reservations, of which he himself is quite aware. He describes Torre Galli as marking the extreme limit of a failing wave of Villanovanism, which passed through Campania and just reached the southern extremity of Italy, but was too weak to cross the straits into Sicily. I do not suggest that the statement is not correct, and it would be almost unexceptionable if it were not for the echoes of outworn theories that a practised ear cannot fail to detect. Orsi himself does not share

these theories, but he seems to me to pay them
somewhat too much deference. The idea that
Villanovanism was directly descended from the
Terremare is debatable. But the theory that it
was the sole civilizing force in the Italy of pre-
Hellenic and pre-Etruscan days can certainly no
longer be entertained. The Villanovans, as I have
shown, were the most important power in all
Northern Italy and a great part of the centre, but
their territorial expansion was strictly limited. It
did not pass south of Monte Circeo, nor east of
the Apennines below the level of Rimini. What
was the general civilization south of Rome in the
Neolithic or the Bronze Age we have no means
as yet of knowing ; there has been no exploration,
except at Molfetta and Matera, on which any
theories could be built. The early Iron Age of
the southern half of the peninsula may well
have evolved from a Bronze Age which has little
relationship to the Terremare. And the direct
connexions with the Iron Age civilization of
Villanova are certainly so slight as to be readily
explicable by a little commercial intercourse.

Torre Galli, which remained much more
Italian in its character than Canale, was naturally
linked to Campania by a line of practicable coast-
roads. It was inevitable that there should be a
certain amount of traffic along these, and that
Campanian products should find their way into

Western Calabria. It is said, for instance, that the pottery is very similar, and this is quite true. But it is surely an exaggeration to point to the use of a water-jar resembling the Villanovan ossuary as a proof of Villanovan influence. Actually it is a proof of how very slight that influence was, for the jar was never used as an ossuary; the Calabrian burial customs were diametrically opposed to those of the Villanovans, and we now know, as will be shown in a moment, that the Calabrians belonged to a totally different race from the Villanovans. Why, then, emphasize this very trifling point concerning a water-jar which might almost be a coincidence? After all, the shape of our teapots is ultimately derived from China, but we have not taken much else from the civilization of that country. Similarly, though it may be true that an identical pattern of razor was employed in Etruria, Bologna, Venetia, and Calabria, it is useful to remember that Sheffield razors are used in many lands where the population can scarcely be supposed to have originated in England, much less in the particular English county of Yorkshire.

The really important point for the student to bear in mind is not that the Calabrians possibly borrowed the knowledge and use of a few common objects from the Villanovans, but that they were totally opposed to them in every essential respect.

The burial customs were different, for the Calabrians never cremated, and this alone might be
a sufficient argument for difference of origin.
But the radical difference is conclusively proved
by Orsi's study of the very peculiar tomb-forms.
Evidence for this point is derived from Canale
and not from Torre Galli, but there is no reason
to suppose that the two groups of tribes, the one
on the west and the other on the east of the
mountain pass, are not of identical stock.

The Villanovans, as I have so frequently stated,
were of transalpine origin, descended from tribes
living on or near the Danube. But the Calabrians
of Torre Galli and Canale were Siculans, close
blood-relatives of the inhabitants of Sicily. This
is one of the most startling of Orsi's discoveries
and may have far-reaching consequences. Various
ancient authors have stated that the Siculans
originally occupied a large part of Italy; which is
perfectly consistent with the view expressed in my
first chapter that the Neolithic population crossed
over from North Africa by way of Sicily. It may
well be that, as discovery proceeds in parts of
South Italy which are still unexplored, we shall
find traces of Siculan occupation over a great part
of the peninsula south of Rome. Orsi has already
noted some very significant hints in widely separated regions.

The main features of the landscape near Canale

are very reminiscent of Sicily. On the command-
ing hill now occupied by the medieval castle of
Gerace rose in the seventh century B.C. the acropolis of the Greek city of Locri. Through the
valley below rushes a tumultuous torrent, and on
the opposite side of the stream rise the steep cliffs
on which the pre-Hellenic natives planted their
villages. The stream-riven hills in this part are
composed of a crumbly sandstone, which lends
itself very naturally to the excavation of rock-
chambers. All the essential characteristics are repeated here which may be seen in the hinterland of Eastern Sicily. Indeed, the view might
almost represent a scene somewhere among the
mountains that rise a few miles back from the
coast between Catania and Siracusa. And so it
seems quite natural, though wholly unexpected,
that the tombs found at Canale should be precisely similar to those which the Siculans of the
Bronze and Iron Ages hewed in the cliffs of Pan-
talica or Finocchito. But this is a unique phenomenon in Italy; not one of the peoples whose
burials have been described in preceding chapters
ever made tombs of this style and character. It
is true that the Etruscans, in the seventh century
and later, cut rock-tombs in the soft tufo of Tuscany. But no Etruscans even landed in Italy for
a full hundred years after the foundation of
Canale, and at no time did they ever penetrate

within many weeks' journey of this Calabrian highland.

Moreover, it is no mere general resemblance that connects the Siculan with the Calabrian rock-tomb; the peculiar plan and arrangement of all the essential parts is identical on each side of the straits. The plan is quite elaborately designed. A fore-court, generally about two metres long and approximately square in shape, forms the vestibule. At its northern end this court narrows to a short passage, completely barred in the middle by a monolithic door of untrimmed stone. Beyond this door is the funeral chamber, an oblong or square room of much the same size as the fore-court or a little larger. Inside the chamber itself a low divan was cut round each side, but the centre of the floor was hollowed out so as to form a depression. The skeletons were generally laid in the hollow, with their heads resting on the ledge, fully extended but with their legs slightly bent. The dead had been buried in their clothes, the men surrounded with their weapons, the women covered with their ornaments, and all alike equipped with quantities of pottery vessels for the water and food that they would require in the next world.

At Torre Galli the difference of the geological structure rendered it impossible to make rock-tombs, for the plateau on which this village stood was composed not of sandstone but of clay. Here, therefore, the Siculans had to do the best that they could with a material quite unsuitable for their traditional forms. This is probably the only reason that trench-graves instead of rock-chambers are found at Torre Galli.

Considering that the inhabitants of these villages in Southern Calabria were the direct blood-relatives of the Siculans across the straits, and that they were only separated from them by a few miles of sea, it is very noteworthy that there was no appreciable intercourse between the two sides of the water. The material civilization of the Calabrians owes nothing to Sicily. This is perhaps the strongest of all the instances of a rule that asserts itself throughout the pre-history of the two countries. Sicily and Italy are always distinct, each working out its own development on its own particular lines without the slightest dependence on the other. The only respect in which they may sometimes be compared is when they are both trading simultaneously with the same places in the Aegean.

At Canale there is evidence that trade with Greece began at a fairly early stage in the Iron Age. This evidence is provided by a series of geometrically painted vases, very similar to those found in Sicily during the eighth and ninth centuries. In Sicily the constant process of importa-

tion produced a distinct local school which will
be mentioned in the next chapter. But at Canale
the native potters were never influenced by the
foreign models, and continued serenely to produce
their old monochrome black ware without appre-
ciably modifying their patterns or their style. It
is very significant that none of the early Greek
ware ever found its way over the mountains to
Torre Galli. The exact moment, indeed, at which
Greek influence began to be at all powerful in
Torre Galli is defined by the pottery on that site.
Corinthian ware appears there, but proto-Corinthian is wholly absent; which shows that commercial relations only began at the end of the
seventh century. From that time onwards there
seems to be a period of peaceful intercourse with
Locri ; which lasted down to the final and successful aggression by the Locrians at the middle or end
of the sixth century.

To a period at Torre Galli preceding the Greek
penetration belongs a whole series of very fine
weapons in bronze and iron, of which some typical
examples are shown in Plate 17. The tribes of this
settlement were of very warlike habit, to judge
from the large number of short swords, daggers,
spears, and javelins found in their tombs. But they
fought without defensive armour, for there are no
helmets, shields, or corselets. The most important
and interesting of their weapons were the swords

with T-shaped hilts. Four of these were of bronze and twelve of iron. The sheaths were made of wood, covered with a thin sheet of metal, either bronze or iron, on which rectilinear designs were engraved. Hilts were covered with bone or ivory, sometimes engraved, and were made for the grasp of an extremely small hand. These swords belong to a group which is widely diffused over Central Italy west of the Apennines, though extremely rare in the north. As they are entirely absent from Canale it is evident that they were not being brought in from Greece at this time, though the origin of the type is ultimately sub-Mycenaean. It must be inferred that the original models came to the west coast of Italy in the ninth, or possibly the tenth, century, and were promptly imitated by local makers who thenceforward supplied the whole market. As more examples of iron are known than of bronze, it is quite likely that the iron-mines of Bruttium supplied the metal.

A fully armed warrior at Torre Galli was normally equipped with spear and javelin as well as with his sword. All these weapons were often found together, but spears were the more numerous (Plate 17, no. 3). At Canale, on the other hand, there were no swords, but spears were very frequent, and were far more often made of iron than the spears of Torre Galli. This may be best explained by supposing that Canale received its iron

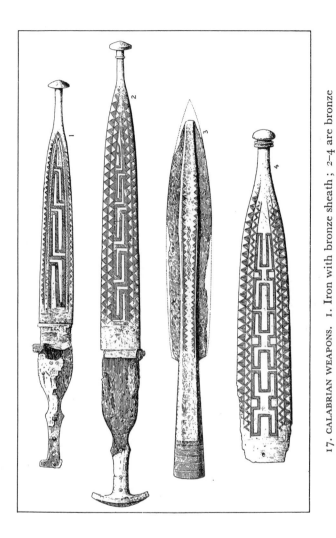

17. CALABRIAN WEAPONS. 1. Iron with bronze sheath; 2–4 are bronze

weapons exclusively from Greek sources, unless the closer proximity of the local iron-mines is to be considered a sufficient explanation.

In respect of ornaments as well as of weapons there are some striking differences between the two sides of the mountains. For instance, at Torre Galli three-quarters of the fibulae were of the simple or slightly thickened bow type. But at Canale the bow only made up a seventh of the whole list of fibulae, while the boat type, practically unknown at Torre Galli, was far the most popular form. This, like many other minor differences, is undoubtedly due to the presence or absence in each case of early Greek influence. We have seen that trade with pre-colonial Greece powerfully affected Canale as early as the ninth and eighth centuries, whereas it had almost no influence over Torre Galli. Boat fibulae are well known in Greece and were probably imported into Canale, whereas Torre Galli used only Italian models. Similarly the torque, well known in Greek tombs of the eighth century, appears at Canale but not at Torre Galli.

In regard to other details of trade it is to be observed that amber was found in fully half the graves of Torre Galli, whereas glass was rather rare; conversely, at Canale there is a considerable amount of glass but much less amber. It is found only in small pieces in these Calabrian graves, which is natural enough considering the immense distance that it had travelled, down from the Baltic to Trieste and then over hundreds of miles of mountain tracks.

No objects of Etruscan manufacture were found at Torre Galli, and no bronze vessels occurred on either site except the familiar small Greek bowls. The most distinctive of all the Villanovan crafts, that of working in hammered plates of metal, was totally unknown in Calabria, as indeed it was unknown anywhere south of the Tiber.

CHAPTER 13

Sicily. A General Review

The complete divorce between Sicily and Italy throughout all prehistoric time. The Neolithic Age in Sicily. Sicani and Siculi. Limits of the several periods. Character of tomb-construction in the First two Siculan periods. Ritual of the funeral feast. Pottery of the First Siculan stage. Mycenaean imports. The fourteenth and thirteenth centuries represent the finest Siculan culture. Italy and Sicily arrived by quite different roads at the high-water mark of their respective civilizations in the Bronze Age.

NOTHING could be more striking, or more unexpected to the ordinary reader of history, than the complete divorce between Italy and Sicily, which began even in the Neolithic times and continued till after the foundation of the Greek colonies. It is as though an ocean instead of a narrow strait divided the two countries. The Stone and Bronze Ages in Sicily exhibit a most interesting local civilization, which does not closely resemble anything else known in the Mediterranean, and is wholly different from the contemporary civilizations of Italy. The same cleavage persists during the first half of the Iron Age; there is not a trace in Sicily of Danubian influence, or of that Hallstatt cycle which permeates almost the whole continent of Europe. Nor has a single object of Etruscan manufacture ever been found in the island. It is conceivable, of course, that exploration in the still unknown regions of Southern Italy may bring to light some unexpected connexion, but the probability of this seems much diminished by the study that was made in the last chapter. Even the native Siculans inhabiting Calabria derived, as we have seen, virtually nothing from their cousins across the straits. Italy forms an integral part of the continental development of European civilization, whereas Sicily seems to belong to a different orbit, in which the islands from Crete to the Balearics may ultimately prove to have a more or less connected unity.

The prehistoric archaeology of Sicily opens with the Neolithic, inasmuch as there is very little certain evidence of Palaeolithic remains. Two distinct currents can be detected in the Neolithic period, which seem to be entirely unconnected, though chronologically very near to one another. The one current is represented by the site of Stentinello near Syracuse, and the other by the products of certain caves near Syracuse and Palermo. It is the pottery found in the caves which chiefly suggests the wide range of Sicilian connexions at this time, inasmuch as it belongs to that far-flung series which includes the well-known bell-shaped cup or beaker. Stentinello, on the other hand, produced a pottery of a wholly different class, which has no very close analogies anywhere

Map of

SOUTHERN ITALY

and part of

SICILY

in the Mediterranean, though it bears a family resemblance to wares found at Molfetta in Apulia. Further researches are needed both in Sicily and other countries before any opinion can safely be expressed as to the origin and connexions of the culture of this period, which is called for convenience the Sicanian.

Whether there is really any meaning in the distinction drawn by classical writers between *Sicani* and *Siculi* is a much-debated point. Archaeologists have agreed to leave the question open, but to adopt the word *Sicanian* as a useful term for the Neolithic while reserving *Siculan* for all the succeeding periods. Accordingly the First Siculan period will be the Chalcolithic, the Second Siculan will include the Bronze Age together with the first two or three centuries of the early Iron Age, while the Third Siculan is defined as from 900 to 700 B.C. After 700 B.C. the native civilization begins to hybridize with the Greek and is completely lost in it before 500 B.C. These are the divisions established by Orsi, to whose explorations our whole knowledge of the pre-Hellenic and most of our knowledge of Hellenic life in Sicily is due.

For the study of the First Siculan period a considerable amount of material is available. Several large and important cemeteries have been explored near Syracuse, on the results of which Professor

T. E. Peet based the account in his well-known book on *The Stone and Bronze Ages in Italy.* Two sites which have been discovered since his work do not in any way modify the conclusions, but only add to the quantity of material. Passing over all the minor varieties, which are fully described in this book, I would call attention only to such a cemetery as Castelluccio. Here we may first make acquaintance with features which are characteristic of all the most representative Siculan cemeteries whatever their period. At Castelluccio the tombs are cut in a vertical face of rock and entered by a short horizontal corridor. This corridor leads into a circular or elliptical chamber which is closed by a large slab of stone.

With the process of time modifications are made in this scheme, but the normal type of construction remains essentially the same if only the geology of the site allows it. In the Second Siculan period the corridor went out of use and was sometimes replaced by an unroofed antechamber. Thus in a typical case at Thapsos (Peet, fig. 228) the antechamber, door, and chamber were arranged on a plan closely resembling that used at Canale as described in the last chapter. Only the Siculans in the Bronze Age were far ahead of the Calabrians of the tenth century B.C. They used, at least in their finer tombs, masonry blocks and stone pillars to receive the door which closed the entrance; and the interior of the chamber in this Second Siculan period was usually roofed in the beehive or tholos form. These differences are plainly due to exactly that contact with the Mycenaean world which Italy never shared. Towards the beginning of the Iron Age the circular form of chamber gradually changed into a rectangular form, which makes the normal tomb of the Third Siculan period precisely like that of Canale at the same date.

Just in the same way that the main lines of tomb construction remained identical, so the religious conceptions which governed the method and style of interment never varied in the First and Second Siculan periods. The idea was to reproduce a funeral feast with all the pomp and circumstance that the time allowed. Accordingly the dead were buried in a squatting position, with large jars beside them to hold water, smaller decorated cups out of which to drink it, and high pottery tables on which the food was placed. The men were of course provided with their weapons, and the women with their ornaments. During the Chalcolithic and the Bronze Ages this ritual was carried out with the utmost elaboration that was possible; the masterpieces of Siculan potters and the rarest imports of the Mycenaean world are found in the tombs. But with the beginning of the Iron Age a gradual degeneration sets in. . The magnificence of the old ritual is relaxed, the idea of the feast is abandoned. In the tenth century the dead were no longer seated at a banquet, but merely laid at full length on the ground with their heads resting on a block of stone. Nor were the objects found with them either valuable or interesting, though in this respect much allowance must be made for the effects of the plundering that took place in the early Middle Ages. Byzantines, Arabs, and others ransacked the ancient graves for metals and removed everything that they could find of value. Enough, however, has survived to show that there was a real deterioration of standard in the early Iron Age. By the tenth century B. C. the native civilization was already beginning to sink into a decadence from which it was only saved by the increasing predominance of Greek influence. Trade and intercourse with Greece of the geometric period can be clearly traced in the ninth century—that is to say, a hundred and fifty years before the foundation of any actual Greek colonies on Sicilian soil.

From 900 to 500 B.C. everything that is of interest in Sicily is either a Greek importation or the direct imitation of a Greek original. The only native invention during the Third period is the hybrid class of Graeco-Siculan pottery.[1]

It is to the Chalcolithic and Bronze Ages,

[1] Illustrated in *The Iron Age in Italy*, Plates 33, 34.

therefore, that we must look for the representative
civilization of the native Siculans; and we find it
to be both brilliant and original even as early as
the First Siculan period. The remarkable characteristic of this Chalcolithic time is the pottery.
I have already remarked that the Sicanians produced a very interesting incised ware, but the
painted pottery of the First Siculan does not seem
to be descended from the Sicanian. It forms a
distinct and peculiar school for which there is no
precise analogy known elsewhere. Peet, searching
for equivalents in any part of the Mediterranean,
has suggested that the nearest connexion is with
the Dimini pottery of Thessaly, a close relative of
which has been found at Molfetta in Apulia. No
better explanation has yet been offered, but the
problem stands almost where it stood twenty years
ago, and little progress has been made towards
its solution. This style appears full-blown in Sicily
at the moment when the latest Neolithic culture
is beginning to pass into that of the earliest Bronze
Age. It is characterized by the use of simple
geometric patterns, almost entirely rectilinear,
painted in dark brown upon a background of
lighter slip. An idea of the principal motives may
be obtained from figs. 77–84 of Peet's book. The
dominant shape is that of an hour-glass, employed
especially for cups; large water-jars with very long
vertical handles, and handsome food-tables stand-

ing as much as 24 inches high, complete the
regular equipment of each tomb. If there is little
positive evidence of extensive trade-connexion
with the Aegean at this early period, the problem
of the pottery is not the only one which suggests
it. The bone ornament found at Castelluccio,
of which more examples have since been found on
other sites (Peet, fig. 75), is virtually identical with
one from the second city of Hissarlik, and must
almost certainly have come from the same place.

Passing from the First to the Second Siculan
period, we find that the full Bronze Age is represented at its best by half a dozen cemeteries
in the neighbourhood of Syracuse, which belong
to the fourteenth and thirteenth centuries. Here
the feature that immediately arrests attention is
the not infrequent appearance of definitely Mycenaean imports. The earliest that occur belong to
the 'Late Minoan third' period for which the
received dating in the Aegean is 1400 to 1200 B.C.
Peet illustrates a fine amphora and a short sword
from the site of Milocca which are the earliest of
the imports, and a very characteristic two-handled
cup and rapier from Cozzo Pantano. Late and
degraded Mycenaean vases belonging to the very
close of the Third Minoan occurred at Thapsos.

All Mycenaean imports disappear before the
end of the Second Siculan period, which is exactly
what would be expected, as this is already the

tenth century B.C., by which time the last echoes of the great Minoan movement have died away everywhere.

It is the fourteenth and thirteenth centuries, therefore, which represent the finest development of the genuine Siculan civilization. This is strongly rooted in the age-old native tradition of the country, but is enriched and vivified by constant trade with the Aegean. Had the great tombs of this period survived intact, their contents would have provided a splendid picture. We may still hope that some day the complete burial of a Siculan chieftain may be discovered. Even from the partial salvage preserved in the museum of Syracuse some idea may be formed of what its riches may have been. Bronze rapiers, swords, and spears, gold rings, bronze mirrors, beads of amber and glass, and ivory combs are only the forgotten débris which the plunderers left behind. Some day we may hope to see the bronze vessels, and perhaps the jewellery, which by a happy chance may have escaped the tomb robber. Not till then, however, shall we know the full magnificence of the Sicilian Bronze Age, which as yet can only be dimly outlined.

In these few pages I have tried not so much to give a sketch of Sicily as to show how different its origin and development were from the Italian. The native civilization in Sicily reached its zenith about 1300 B.C., when Italy also was at the highest point of its Bronze Age development. But the two countries had arrived at their respective goals by very different roads. The Italians had first served an apprenticeship to Hungary and Bohemia, and then raised themselves to a position of more than equality with their teachers. The Sicilians, on the other hand, unconscious of anything that was happening on the continent of Europe, and quite without interest in it, had been drawn into the orbit of the Cretan thalassocracy. It was from commerce with the Aegean that they derived the springs of their inspiration, so that when the Mycenaean power collapsed Sicily lost all her energy. But those very centuries which exhibit the slow decadence of native Sicilian culture are marked in Italy by the rise of strong and youthful nations. Building on a continuous foundation of inherited knowledge and experience, the Italians of the Iron Age acquired ever fresh vigour and independence. Villanovans, Atestines, Picenes, and others, even before the coming of Etruscans and Greeks, had built up the greatness of provincial Italy. By the fourth century it was a country civilized from end to end and ready for its political unification under the Romans. The independent vigour and energy of its several peoples and provinces made the ultimate strength and coherence of the Roman state.

INDEX